Story Collection
5 Stories
3

Disney·Pixar Story Collection 3

초판 발행 · 2022년 11월 22일 | **발행인** · 이종원 | **발행처** · 길벗스쿨
주소 · 서울시 마포구 월드컵로 10길 56(서교동) | **대표 전화** · 02)332-0931 | **팩스** · 02) 323-0586
홈페이지 · www.gilbutschool.co.kr | **이메일** · gilbutschool@gilbut.co.kr
기획 및 책임편집 · 이경희(natura@gilbut.co.kr), 한슬기, 임채원 | **디자인** · 이현숙 | **제작** · 이준호, 손일순, 이진혁
영업마케팅 · 김진성, 박선경 | **웹마케팅** · 박달님, 권은나 | **영업관리** · 정경화 | **독자지원** · 윤정아, 최희창
한글 번역 · 최주연 | **영문 감수** · Ryan P. Lagace | **전산편집** · 연디자인 | **녹음** · YR미디어 | **CTP 출력 및 인쇄** · 교보피앤비 | **제본** · 경문제책

▶ 잘못 만든 책은 구입한 서점에서 바꿔 드립니다.
▶ 이 책은 저작권법에 따라 보호받는 저작물이므로 무단전재와 무단복제를 금합니다.
　이 책의 전부 또는 일부를 이용하려면 반드시 사전에 저작권자와 길벗스쿨의 서면 동의를 받아야 합니다.

ISBN 979-11-6406-450-2 64740 (길벗 도서번호 30517)
　　　 979-11-6406-447-2 64740 (세트)

Copyright©2022 Disney Enterprises, Inc. and Pixar. All rights reserved.

정가 22,000원

CONTENTS

Story Collection 3

1. **Moana** ········· 7~34
2. **Coco** ········· 35~62
3. **Incredibles 2** ········· 63~90
4. **Zootopia** ········· 91~118
5. **Frozen 2** ········· 119~146

COMPONENTS

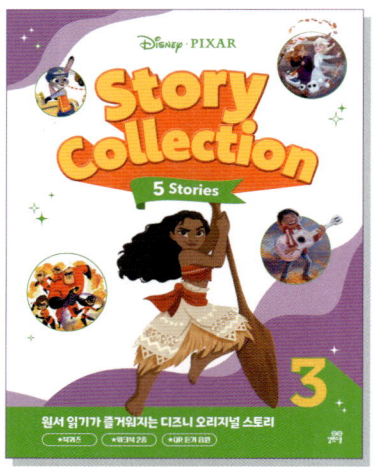

Main Book
5 popular stories based on Disney movies

인기 많은 디즈니 애니메이션 영화 5편의 내용을 한 권에 담은 콜렉션입니다. 영화 장면을 생동감 있게 표현한 일러스트와 오리지널 스토리를 가장 충실하게 녹여낸 문장으로, 원서 읽는 즐거움뿐만 아니라 영어 실력까지 향상시킬 수 있습니다.

Characters & Key Words

알아두면 원서 읽기가 쉬워지는 단어들을 선별했습니다. 등장인물들의 이름 표기와 맥락 이해에 중요한 역할을 하는 키워드 40개를 학습해 보세요.

캐릭터

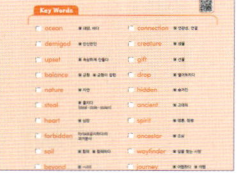
키워드

MP3 Audio Files

QR코드를 스캔하면 아래의 음원을 들으면서 학습할 수 있습니다. 스트리밍 듣기 또는 전체 파일 다운로드가 가능합니다.
- Key Words
- Story Reading

바로 듣기

길벗스쿨 e클래스
eclass.gilbut.co.kr → 학습 자료실

Activity Book
Includes book quizzes, questions for words, sentences, details and reading skills

스토리를 읽고 나서 얼마나 잘 이해했는지 진단하는 북 퀴즈를 제공합니다. 15개의 문제를 풀어 보고, 맞힌 개수를 확인해 보세요.
액티비티 파트에서는 다양한 유형의 연습문제를 접하며 단어, 문장 구성, 세부적인 내용 이해뿐만 아니라 글의 전체 구조까지 파악하는 힘을 기를 수 있습니다.

Word Check

Story Check

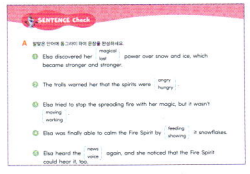
Sentence Check

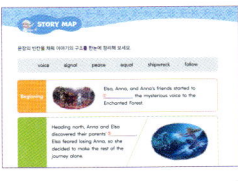
Story Map

Practice Book
for word & sentence practice

어휘력과 문장력을 강화하는 연습용 워크북이 제공됩니다. 각 장면에 등장하는 어휘의 철자와 뜻을 정확히 익히는 단어 연습장과 빈칸을 채워 문장을 완성하는 문장 완성 연습장으로 이뤄집니다. 문장 완성 연습장은 본책 스토리의 우리말 뜻을 확인하는 해석본으로 사용할 수 있습니다.

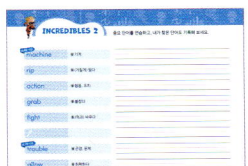
Word Practice

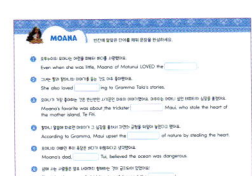
Sentence Practice

HOW TO READ

영어 실력이 한 단계 업그레이드 되는 원서 읽기

Step 1. 워밍업, 키워드 살펴보기

책을 읽기 전, 내용 파악에 핵심적인 역할을 하는 단어들을 미리 살펴보세요. 스토리에 등장하는 주요 캐릭터들의 이름을 확인하고, 내용을 예측해 봅니다.

Step 2. 집중 듣기

손으로 단어를 짚어가면서 원어민 성우의 음성을 귀 기울여 들어 보세요. 이런 집중 듣기를 통해 낯선 단어가 어떻게 발음되는지 정확하게 알 수 있으며, 음원의 속도에 맞추어 눈으로 읽어 내려가는 연습을 하다 보면 많은 양의 글을 빠르고 정확하게 읽을 수 있는 능력이 길러집니다.

Step 3. 소리 내어 읽기

소리 내어 읽어 보세요. 소리 내어 읽을 때 눈으로 보는 텍스트와 귀로 듣는 소리가 연계가 되고, 반복하여 읽을수록 읽는 속도와 정확성이 향상됩니다. 이런 과정에서 단어와 문장 구조를 인지할 수 있고, 뜻을 기억해내며 독해력을 발달시킬 수 있습니다.

Step 4. 북퀴즈로 이해도 확인하기

스토리의 내용을 얼마나 파악했는지 북퀴즈를 풀어 점검해 보세요. 맞힌 개수가 적다면 스토리북을 꼼꼼히 다시 읽으면서 정확히 이해할 수 있도록 합니다.

Step 5. 워크북 학습하기

Activity Book을 풀이하며 스토리의 세부내용을 살펴보고, 스토리에 담긴 영어 표현과 문장 구조를 익히는 시간을 가져 보세요.
또한 Practice Book을 통해 어려웠던 단어나 의미를 분명히 알지 못했던 단어를 별도로 학습하며 어휘력을 높이고, 문장 하나 하나의 정확한 의미를 확인해 보세요.

Characters

Moana

Gramma Tala

Maui

Tamatoa

Te Kā

Te Fiti

Key Words

- ocean 명 대양, 바다
- demigod 명 반신반인
- upset 동 속상하게 만들다
- balance 명 균형 형 균형이 잡힌
- nature 명 자연
- steal 동 훔치다 (steal - stole - stolen)
- heart 명 심장
- forbidden forbid(금지하다)의 과거분사
- sail 명 항해 동 항해하다
- beyond 전 ~너머
- connection 명 연관성, 연결
- creature 명 생물
- gift 명 선물
- drop 동 떨어트리다
- hidden 형 숨겨진
- ancient 형 고대의
- spirit 명 영혼, 정령
- ancestor 명 조상
- wayfinder 명 길을 찾는 사람
- journey 동 여행하다 명 여행

Key Words

- [ ] **restore** 통 복구하다
- [ ] **storm** 명 폭풍
- [ ] **faraway** 형 멀리 떨어진
- [ ] **expect** 통 예상하다, 기대하다
- [ ] **promise** 통 약속하다
- [ ] **fishhook** 명 닻걸이
- [ ] **get past** ~의 곁을 지나가다
- [ ] **dive** 통 다이빙하다
- [ ] **trick** 통 속이다
- [ ] **retrieve** 통 되찾다
- [ ] **current** 명 해류, 흐름
- [ ] **navigate** 통 길을 찾다, 항해하다
- [ ] **lava** 명 용암
- [ ] **defeat** 통 ~를 물리치다
- [ ] **courage** 명 용기
- [ ] **meant** mean(의미하다)의 과거형, 과거분사
- [ ] **bloom** 통 꽃을 피우다
- [ ] **transform** 통 바뀌다, 변형하다
- [ ] **hawk** 명 매
- [ ] **leader** 명 지도자, 대표

Adapted by
Laura Hitchcock

Illustrated by
Griselda Sastrawinata-Lemay

Designed by
Tony Fejeran

A special thanks to the wonderful people of the Pacific Islands for inspiring us on this journey as we bring the world of Moana *to life.*

Even when she was little, Moana of Motunui LOVED the ocean.

She also loved listening to Gramma Tala's stories. Moana's favorite was about the trickster **demigod Maui**, who stole the heart of the mother island, Te Fiti.

According to Gramma, Maui upset the **balance of nature** by stealing the heart.

Moana's dad, Chief Tui, believed the ocean was dangerous. The islanders were forbidden to sail beyond the reef!

But little Moana felt a deep connection to the ocean, and to all the creatures who belonged in it. She always wanted to help.

And the ocean noticed! It gave Moana a **special gift.**

When Chief Tui picked up Moana, she dropped the gift.

Luckily, someone else picked it up.

It was Gramma Tala! She believed the ocean's gift was the heart of

Te Fiti!

As she grew, Moana worked hard to help lead her people and follow her father's rules. But when Moana turned sixteen, Gramma Tala took her aside. "It's time to learn who you were meant to be," Gramma said. She led Moana to a hidden cavern . . .

. . . full of **ancient canoes**.

When Moana started drumming,

Bam! Bam! Bam!

she could feel the spirits of her ancestors. They were *wayfinders*—voyagers on the ocean!

Gramma Tala's last wish was for Moana to journey across the ocean, find Maui, and restore the heart of Te Fiti.

So, with the heart safe inside her necklace, Moana set sail.

But sailing on the open ocean was not easy for Moana—especially when a **storm** hit!

Moana and her boat washed up on a faraway island, where she met

Maui the demigod!

He was NOT what Moana expected.

Maui stole Moana's boat!
But when he tried to sail away, the ocean made sure Moana went with him.

The ocean wanted them to work together.

Maui promised to help return the heart of Te Fiti ONLY if Moana helped him find his **magic fishhook**.

But first, they had to get past the **Kakamora**, an army of wild, coconut-clad bandits.

Along the way, Maui taught Moana how to wayfind, which is to use the **sun**, the **stars**,

the **moon**,

and the **ocean current** to navigate.

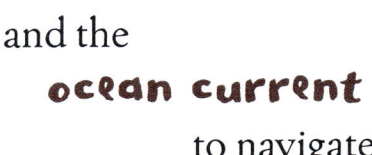

And when the journey became too difficult, the spirit of Gramma Tala returned. "Know who you are meant to be," Gramma's spirit told Moana.

When Moana and Maui finally reached Te Fiti, the mother island was gone. Instead, there was a *lava monster* named Te Kā!

Summoning all her **courage**, Moana gave the heart to Te Kā. And Te Kā remembered who she was meant to be. . . .

She was **Te Fiti!**
With her heart restored, Te Fiti **bloomed** once again.
The world was back in balance.

Moana and Maui said goodbye. Their journey together was complete.

Maui transformed into a **hawk** and flew away.

It was time for Moana to return to her people.

The young girl from Motunui now knew exactly who she was meant to be.

She was a **daughter**, a **leader**, and a **wayfinder**.

She was Moana!

Characters

Dante

Miguel

Héctor

Ernesto

Mamá Coco

Mamá Imelda

Abuelita

Key Words

- [ ] full — 형 가득한
- [ ] memory — 명 기억
- [ ] relative — 명 친척
- [ ] pass on — 돌아가시다
- [ ] musician — 명 음악가
- [ ] rule — 명 규칙
- [ ] husband — 명 남편
- [ ] inspired — 형 영감을 받은
- [ ] tumble — 동 굴러 떨어지다
- [ ] discovery — 명 발견

- [ ] familiar — 형 익숙한, 친숙한
- [ ] tomb — 명 무덤
- [ ] hung — hang(매달다)의 과거형
- [ ] mad — 형 몹시 화가 난
- [ ] strum — 명 (현악기를) 퉁기기
- [ ] skeleton — 명 해골
- [ ] path — 명 길
- [ ] petal — 명 꽃잎
- [ ] blessing — 명 축복
- [ ] team up — 팀을 짜다

Key Words

- [ ] **polish** 명 광택제 / 동 윤을 내다
- [ ] **perform** 동 공연하다, 연주하다
- [ ] **ditch** 동 버리다
- [ ] **fiesta** 명 축제
- [ ] **crowded** 형 붐비는, 복잡한
- [ ] **fell** fall(빠지다)의 과거형
- [ ] **overjoyed** 형 매우 기뻐하는
- [ ] **argue** 동 언쟁하다
- [ ] **truth** 명 진실
- [ ] **poison** 동 독살하다 / 명 독

- [ ] **stolen** steal(훔치다)의 과거분사
- [ ] **threw** throw(던지다)의 과거형
- [ ] **pit** 명 구덩이
- [ ] **lullaby** 명 자장가
- [ ] **unidentified** 형 정체불명의
- [ ] **rescue** 명 구출 / 동 구출하다
- [ ] **disappear** 동 사라지다
- [ ] **forget** 동 잊어버리다
- [ ] **remind** 동 (기억하도록) 상기시키다
- [ ] **support** 명 지원, 도움

Adapted by
Adrian Molina

Illustrated by
Fabiola Garza

Designed by
Tony Fejeran

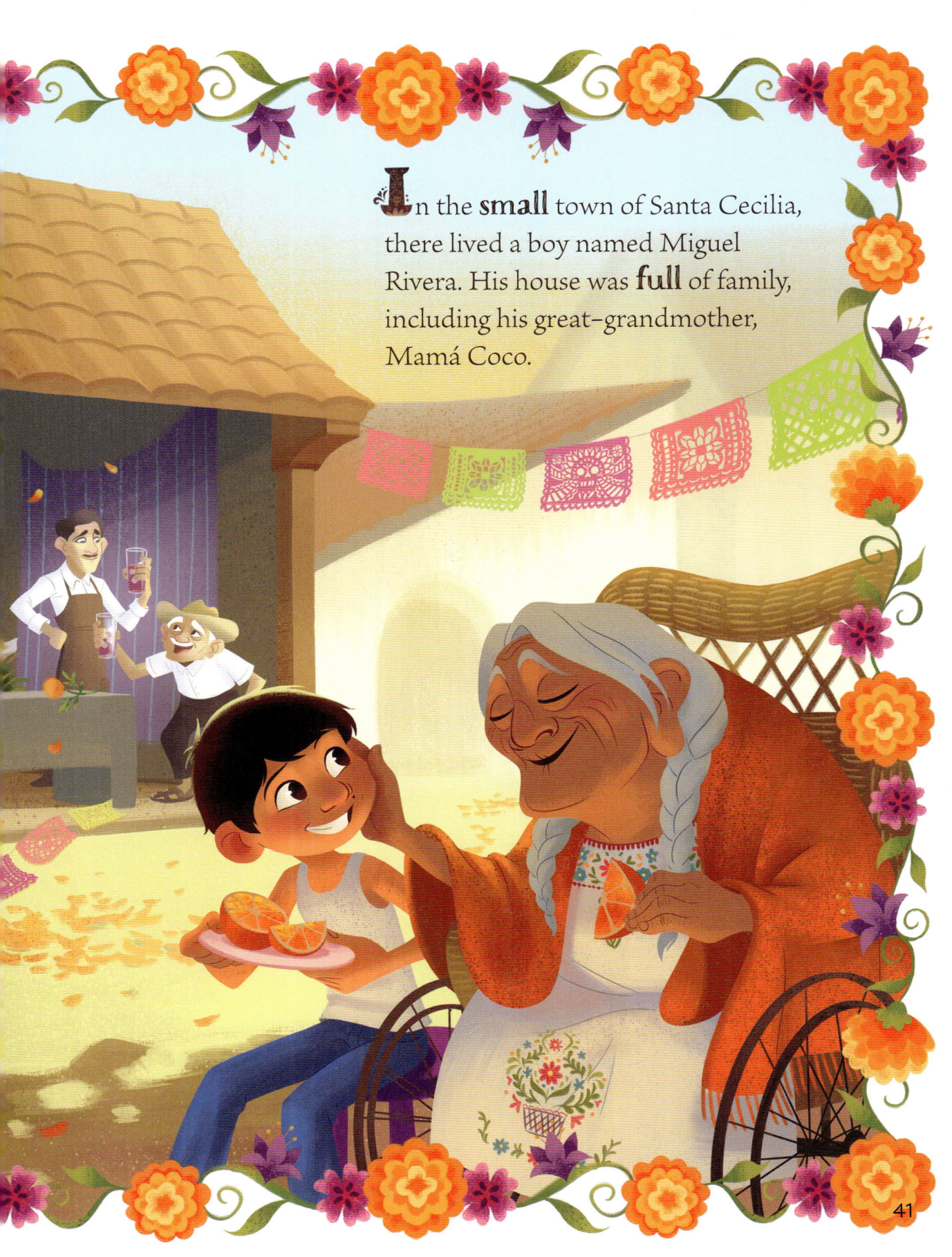

In the **small** town of Santa Cecilia, there lived a boy named Miguel Rivera. His house was **full** of family, including his great-grandmother, Mamá Coco.

Every year on Día de los Muertos, the Day of the Dead, his family shared the **memories** of relatives who had passed on.

Miguel's abuelita would tell the story of his great-great-grandmother, Mamá Imelda, whose heart had been **broken** by her musician husband. Because of him, there was one rule in the Rivera household: NO MUSIC!

But Miguel LOVED music. In his secret hideout, he learned to play guitar by watching videos of his favorite musician, Ernesto de la Cruz.

Feeling inspired and brave, Miguel and his dog, Dante, snuck out of the house to perform in a local talent show.

But on the way out, Dante **jumped** onto the family ofrenda, or altar. Mamá Imelda's photo **tumbled** down with a

crash!

That was when Miguel made a **discovery**. Mamá Imelda's husband was holding a guitar— and it looked very familiar!

"Mamá Coco's papá was **Ernesto de la Cruz!**" Miguel cried. "I'm going to be a **musician!**"

But because of their family rule, his abuelita took his guitar and destroyed it.

SMASH!

Miguel ran as FAST as he could to Ernesto's tomb, where the famous guitar still hung. Taking it off the wall, he said, "Please don't be mad. I need this to be a musician like you!" And he gave the legend's guitar a strum.

All of a sudden, Miguel noticed all the **SKELETONS!** They had followed the path of marigold petals to visit their living relatives for **Día de los Muertos**.

To return to the Land of the Living, Miguel would need a **blessing** from one of his dead family members. So he and Dante crossed the Marigold Bridge into the **Land of the Dead**.

Miguel found Mamá Imelda, but she said she wouldn't give him her blessing if he wanted to be a **musician**. Miguel had to find another way.

So he teamed up with a skeleton named **Héctor**, who said he knew Ernesto de la Cruz.

With some shoe polish, Héctor made Miguel look like a **skeleton**.

They traveled all over looking for Ernesto. They even performed together in a **talent show**!

But Miguel was running out of time. If he didn't get Ernesto's blessing soon, he'd turn into a **REAL** skeleton and never get home!

So he **ditched** Héctor to find his great-great-grandpa on his own.

Miguel snuck into Ernesto's fiesta at the **tippy-top** of a tall tower. But the place was so **crowded**, Miguel couldn't get to Ernesto.

So Miguel belted out a song! Everyone watched as he sang . . . and **fell** into Ernesto's pool.

Splash!

The skeletons saw that he was a **living boy**.

Ernesto was **overjoyed**!

"I have a great-great-grandson!"

But then Héctor appeared, and as the two men argued, Miguel learned the **dark truth**.

His great-great-grandpa had **poisoned** Héctor and **stolen** his songs to become famous.

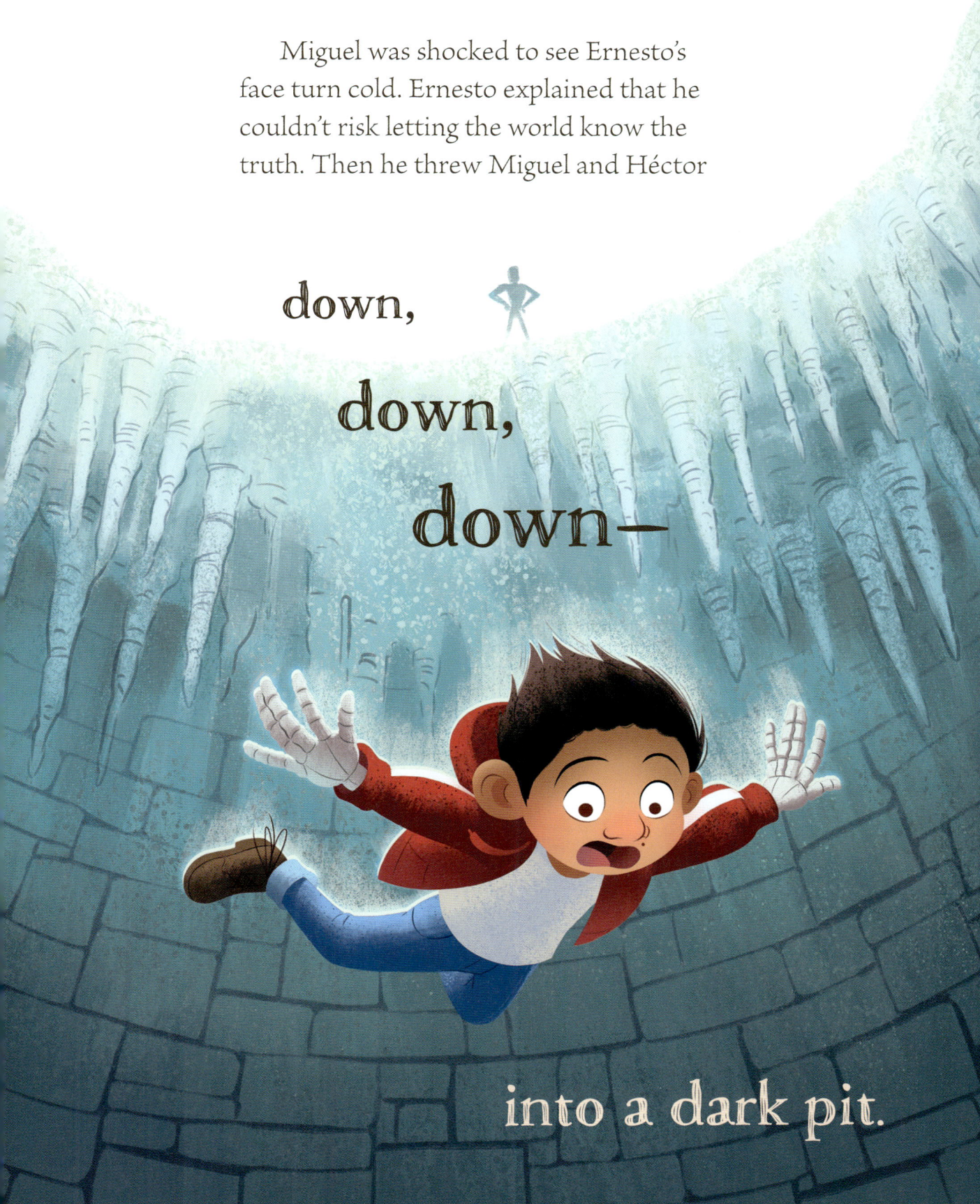

Miguel was shocked to see Ernesto's face turn cold. Ernesto explained that he couldn't risk letting the world know the truth. Then he threw Miguel and Héctor

down,

down,

down—

into a dark pit.

Héctor told Miguel that the songs he'd written were all for his **family**. And there was a special **lullaby** he would always sing for his daughter, Coco.

Miguel thought of Mamá Imelda's photo and the unidentified man. "**It's you!** Héctor, **YOU** are my great-great-grandpa!"

Suddenly, Mamá Imelda and Dante came to their **rescue**.

But Héctor began to **disappear**. His daughter was starting to **forget** him.

Mamá Imelda and Héctor sent Miguel **home** with their blessing.

Back in the Land of the Living, Miguel rushed to Mamá Coco. He sang **"Remember Me"** to remind her of her papá. She typically didn't talk much so Miguel was thrilled when she began to sing along!

Mamá Coco kept her **papá's** memory alive by sharing stories of him with her relatives. At last, the Riveras realized that music could bring them closer together.

And now Miguel knew he could follow his dream and become a musician—with his family's **support**.

Characters

 Mr. Incredible

 Elastigirl

 Jack-Jack

 Violet

 Dash

 Evelyn

 Winston

 Frozone

Key Words

- [ ] rip — 통 (거칠게) 찢다
- [ ] action — 명 행동, 조치
- [ ] grab — 통 붙잡다
- [ ] trouble — 명 곤란, 곤경
- [ ] allow — 통 허락하다
- [ ] undercover — 형 잠복한, 위장한
- [ ] propose — 통 제안하다
- [ ] legal — 형 합법적인
- [ ] assignment — 명 임무
- [ ] spot — 통 발견하다
- [ ] scramble — 통 재빨리 움직이다
- [ ] zoom — 통 (아주 빨리) 휭 하고 가다
- [ ] zip — 통 쌩 하고 가다
- [ ] stretch — 통 뻗다, 늘이다
- [ ] parachute — 명 낙하산
- [ ] exhausted — 형 지쳐버린, 소모된
- [ ] nap — 통 낮잠을 자다
- [ ] criminal — 명 범인, 범죄자
- [ ] commotion — 명 소란, 소동
- [ ] rescue — 명 구출 통 구출하다

Key Words

- [ ] villain — 명 악당
- [ ] attack — 동 공격하다
- [ ] ambassador — 명 대사
- [ ] capture — 동 포획하다
- [ ] destroy — 동 파괴하다
- [ ] spell — 명 마법, 주문
- [ ] uncontrollable — 형 통제할 수 없는
- [ ] hypnotize — 동 최면을 걸다
- [ ] pounce — 동 갑자기 덤벼들다
- [ ] whisk — 동 재빨리 가져가다

- [ ] force — 동 강요하다
- [ ] wicked — 형 사악한
- [ ] crash — 명 충돌 동 충돌하다
- [ ] free — 동 풀어 주다 형 자유로운
- [ ] fierce — 형 사나운, 난폭한
- [ ] opponent — 명 상대, 반대자
- [ ] shore — 명 해변
- [ ] grateful — 형 고마워하는
- [ ] law — 명 법
- [ ] challenge — 명 도전

Incredibles 2

Adapted by
SUZANNE FRANCIS

Illustrated by
SATOSHI HASHIMOTO

Designed by
TONY FEJERAN

The Incredibles were a **FAMILY OF SUPERS**. When a machine started ripping up the city, they sprang into action! While Mr. Incredible and Elastigirl tried to stop it, their kids Violet and Dash grabbed baby Jack-Jack. Their friend Frozone joined in the fight!

The Incredibles stopped the machine but got in big trouble. Supers were not allowed to use their powers. Mr. Incredible and Elastigirl had no choice but to return to their **UNDERCOVER LIVES** as Bob and Helen Parr, along with their kids.

But then a wealthy businessman named Winston Deavor and his sister, Evelyn, proposed a plan to make Supers legal again. Elastigirl would get the first assignment. She was nervous, but this was her chance to help her family—
AND ALL SUPERS.

I LOVE SUPERHEROES!

Winston was so excited to work with Elastigirl, he allowed her whole family to stay in one of his mansions. **DASH LOVED IT!** He used a remote control to move the floors and turn on the waterfalls.

On Elastigirl's first day at her new job, she spotted a runaway train! She hopped onto her Elasticycle and chased the train through the city.

She **SCRAMBLED** over rooftops . . .

. . . **ZOOMED** up a crane . . .

. . . and **ZIPPED** through a tunnel . . .

. . . until finally, she **STRETCHED** into a parachute and slowed down the train—right before it ran off the tracks!

Back at home, Bob was exhausted. Helping with homework, changing diapers, and dealing with teenage drama really knocked him out.

While Bob was napping, Jack-Jack watched TV. Then he heard a **NOISE** in the backyard.

It was an intruder! Jack-Jack tried to stop the criminal.

Bob heard the commotion and ran outside. He couldn't believe his eyes.

"You . . . have . . . **POWERS**!"

The next day, the city buzzed with the news of Elastigirl's amazing rescue. During her first TV interview, a super villain called the **SCREENSLAVER** attacked. He took over an ambassador's helicopter. Elastigirl raced off . . .

. . . and **RESCUED** the ambassador!

Elastigirl still needed to catch the Screenslaver. With Evelyn's help, she traced the villain's signal to his lair. She chased him through the building and **CAPTURED** him!

But something didn't feel right. Elastigirl realized she'd caught the wrong person—Evelyn Deavor was the *real* Screenslaver! Evelyn wanted to destroy her brother's plan and make sure Supers were never legal again. In a flash, Evelyn put **HYPNO-GOGGLES** on Elastigirl! She was under Evelyn's spell.

Meanwhile, Bob needed some serious help with Jack-Jack. The baby's powers were **UNCONTROLLABLE**!

Bob brought him to the smartest person he knew: Edna Mode. Edna made a special **SUPERSUIT** and tracker to help manage Jack-Jack's powers.

Everything was finally calm at home. Then Evelyn called and said Elastigirl was in **TROUBLE**! Bob asked Frozone to watch the kids and then rushed away.

When Mr. Incredible arrived at the Deavors' ship, a hypnotized Elastigirl pounced on him! She fought him until she could put hypno-goggles over his eyes.

Meanwhile, a group of hypnotized Supers arrived to capture the kids. Frozone showed up just in time to help. Dash clicked a remote, and—**ZOOOOM**!—the amazing **INCREDIBILE** pulled up! It whisked the kids away while Frozone was captured by the Supers.

The Incredibile brought the kids to the ship. But where was Jack-Jack? Dash and Violet were tracking their lost brother when a hypnotized Super **ATTACKED**!

Violet flung razor-sharp force fields at the Super until she and Dash could escape.

Everyone on board was under Evelyn's **WICKED SPELL**. She forced the Supers to set the ship on a crash course toward the city.

Suddenly, the kids appeared. They **FREED** their parents and Frozone from the hypnosis. The family was ready to fight together!

The Incredibles and Frozone battled the rest of the hypnotized Supers. Before long, everyone was back to normal.

Then Evelyn tried to escape! Elastigirl chased after her. Evelyn was a **FIERCE OPPONENT**, but she was no match for Elastigirl.

All the Supers **WORKED TOGETHER** to keep the ship from crashing into the city center. They turned the ship around, stopping it just before it reached the shore!

Everyone was grateful to the Supers. The city changed the law, making it legal for them to use their powers again.

Now the Incredibles were ready to face any challenge—**AS A FAMILY**!

Characters

Judy Hopps

Nick

Bogo

Bellwether

Mr. Otterton

Key Words

- [ ] equal — 형 동등한
- [ ] shape — 명 모양
- [ ] claw — 명 발톱
- [ ] achieve — 동 달성하다, 성취하다
- [ ] assignment — 명 임무
- [ ] solve — 동 (문제·곤경을) 해결하다
- [ ] crime — 명 범죄
- [ ] alert — 동 알리다
- [ ] expired — 형 만료된
- [ ] treat — 명 간식
- [ ] desperate — 형 간절히 필요로 하는
- [ ] trick — 동 속이다 명 속임수
- [ ] resold — 동 되팔다
- [ ] profit — 명 이익
- [ ] disappoint — 동 실망시키다
- [ ] case — 명 (경찰이 조사 중인) 사건
- [ ] convince — 동 설득하다, 납득시키다
- [ ] record — 동 녹음하다
- [ ] shady — 형 수상한
- [ ] gather — 동 모으다

Key Words

- [ ] clue — 명 단서, 실마리
- [ ] otter — 명 수달
- [ ] wild — 형 야생의, 사나운
- [ ] prove — 동 증명하다
- [ ] savage — 형 야만적인, 몹시 사나운
- [ ] abandoned — 형 버려진
- [ ] distract — 동 주의를 돌리다
- [ ] slip — 동 슬며시 가다
- [ ] laboratory — 명 실험실
- [ ] ram — 명 숫양
- [ ] mammal — 명 포유동물
- [ ] corner — 동 구석에 가두다
- [ ] sneaky — 형 교활한
- [ ] fang — 명 송곳니
- [ ] predator — 명 포식자
- [ ] sank — sink(주저앉다)의 과거형
- [ ] switch — 동 바꾸다
- [ ] evidence — 명 증거
- [ ] arrest — 동 체포하다
- [ ] cure — 동 치유하다

Disney
ZOOTOPIA

Adapted by
Heather Knowles

Illustrated by
Vivien Wu

Designed by
Alfred Giuliani

Zootopia was an amazing city! Animals of all different sizes and shapes lived and worked together happily. Everyone was equal, whether they had **long claws** or little **paws**.

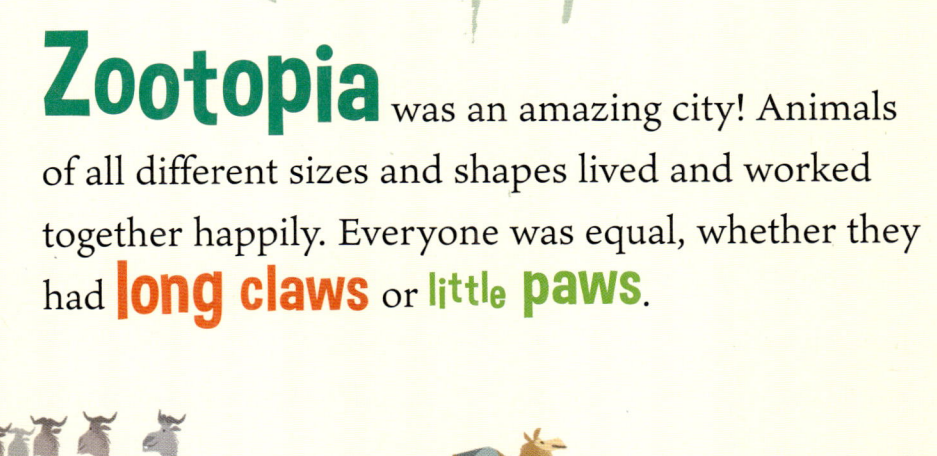

ANYONE CAN BE ANYTHING!

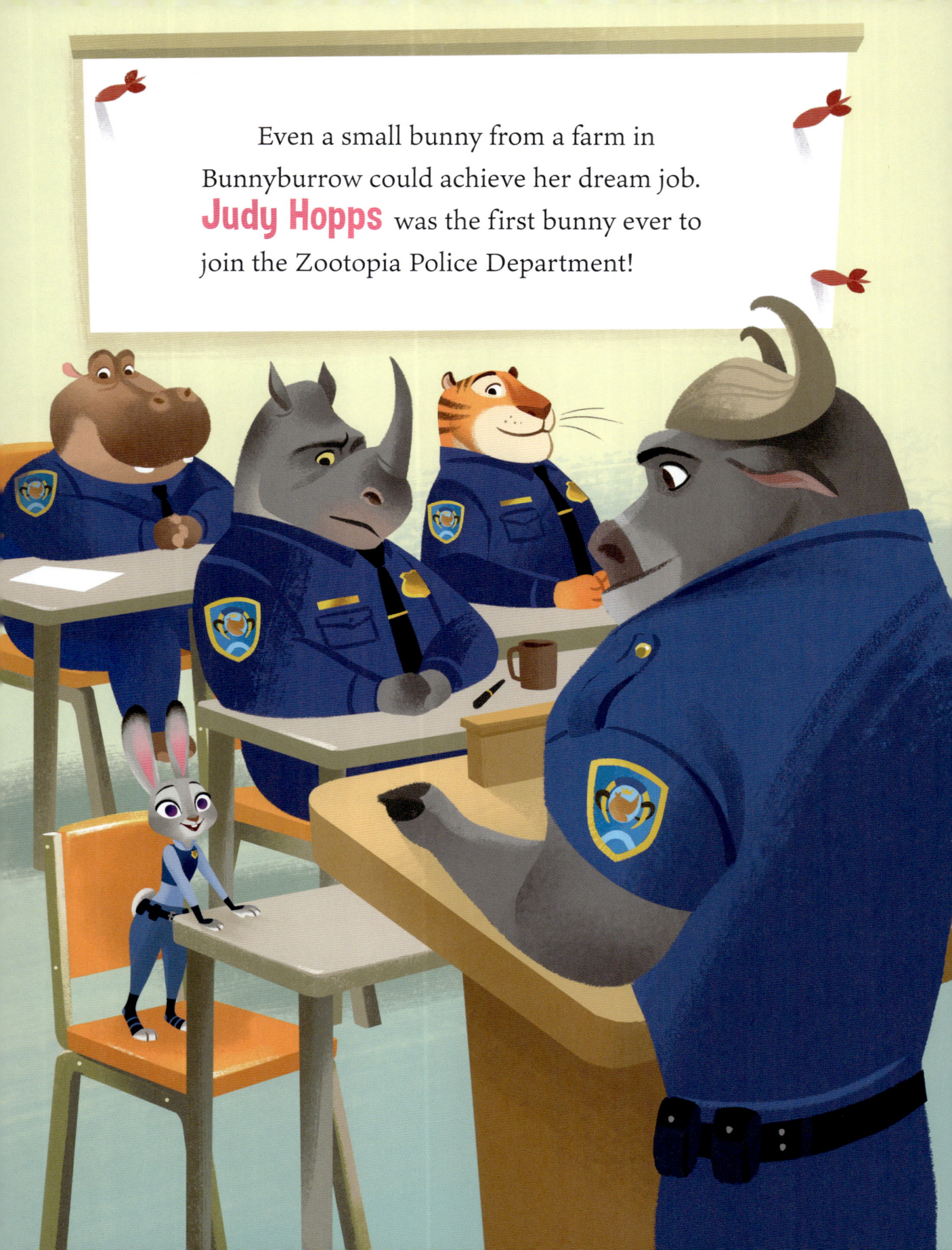

Even a small bunny from a farm in Bunnyburrow could achieve her dream job. **Judy Hopps** was the first bunny ever to join the Zootopia Police Department!

Judy **hopped** with excitement as she waited for her first assignment.

But when Police Chief Bogo handed her a machine for issuing **parking tickets**, her ears **fell**. She wanted to solve crimes, not be a **meter maid**.

Still, Judy wanted to do a good job. Her **sharp hearing** alerted her to expired meters, and she wrote hundreds of parking tickets—before lunchtime!

At noon, Judy headed to a nearby cafe for an **elephant-sized** treat. There she met a little fox who was desperate for a Jumbo-pop. His dad, **Nick**, was out of cash, so Judy offered to pay.

But very soon, Judy learned that Nick had **tricked** her!

He melted the **Jumbo-pop**...

... to create **smaller pawpsicles**.

Then he resold those for a **big profit**!

That night, Judy went to bed **disappointed**. The day hadn't turned out like she'd planned. She wanted to **fight crime**.

I JUST NEED ONE CHANCE . . .

The next day, Judy got her chance. Mrs. Otterton's husband was missing, and Judy offered to take the case. Assistant Mayor Bellwether agreed, and Mrs. Otterton was so grateful! But Judy had only **two days** to solve the crime!

Judy learned that Nick had seen Mr. Otterton recently. She convinced the fox to help her by pulling her own trick: she used her **carrot pen** to record him talking about his shady business deals!

Reluctantly, Nick helped Judy gather clues all across **Zootopia** . . . until they reached the Rainforest District. The plan was to question **Mr. Manchas**, the last animal to have seen the otter.

Nick and Judy found Mr. Manchas, but something was **wrong** with him.

He had gone **WILD**!

Nick and Judy worked together and escaped. They were becoming **friends**! Both of them wanted to solve this case and prove they could do important work.

Judy knew how to find their next lead! Using security camera footage, she led Nick to a **scary building** on the edge of town.

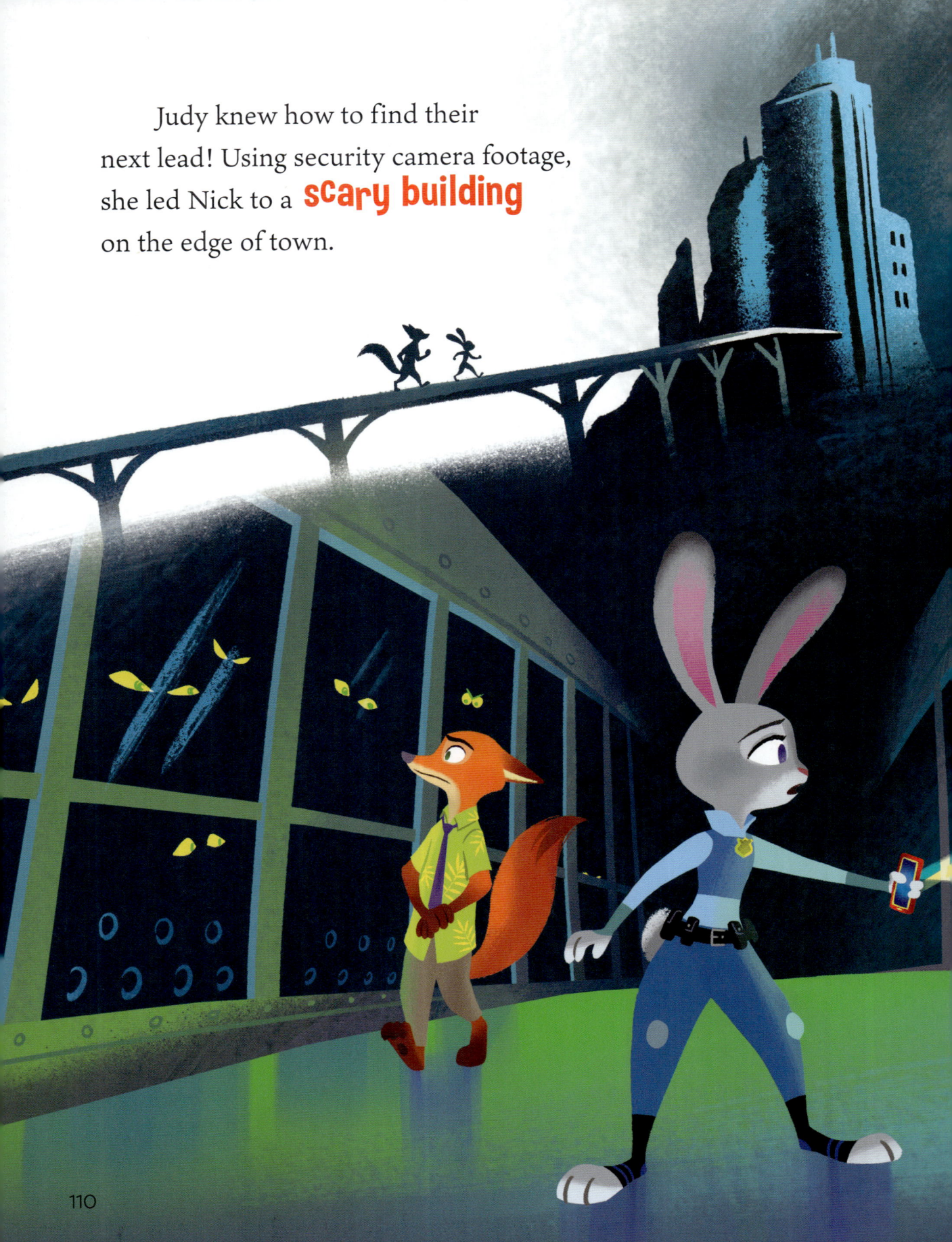

Inside, they found more wild-eyed animals—including the missing otter! Why had these animals turned **savage**?

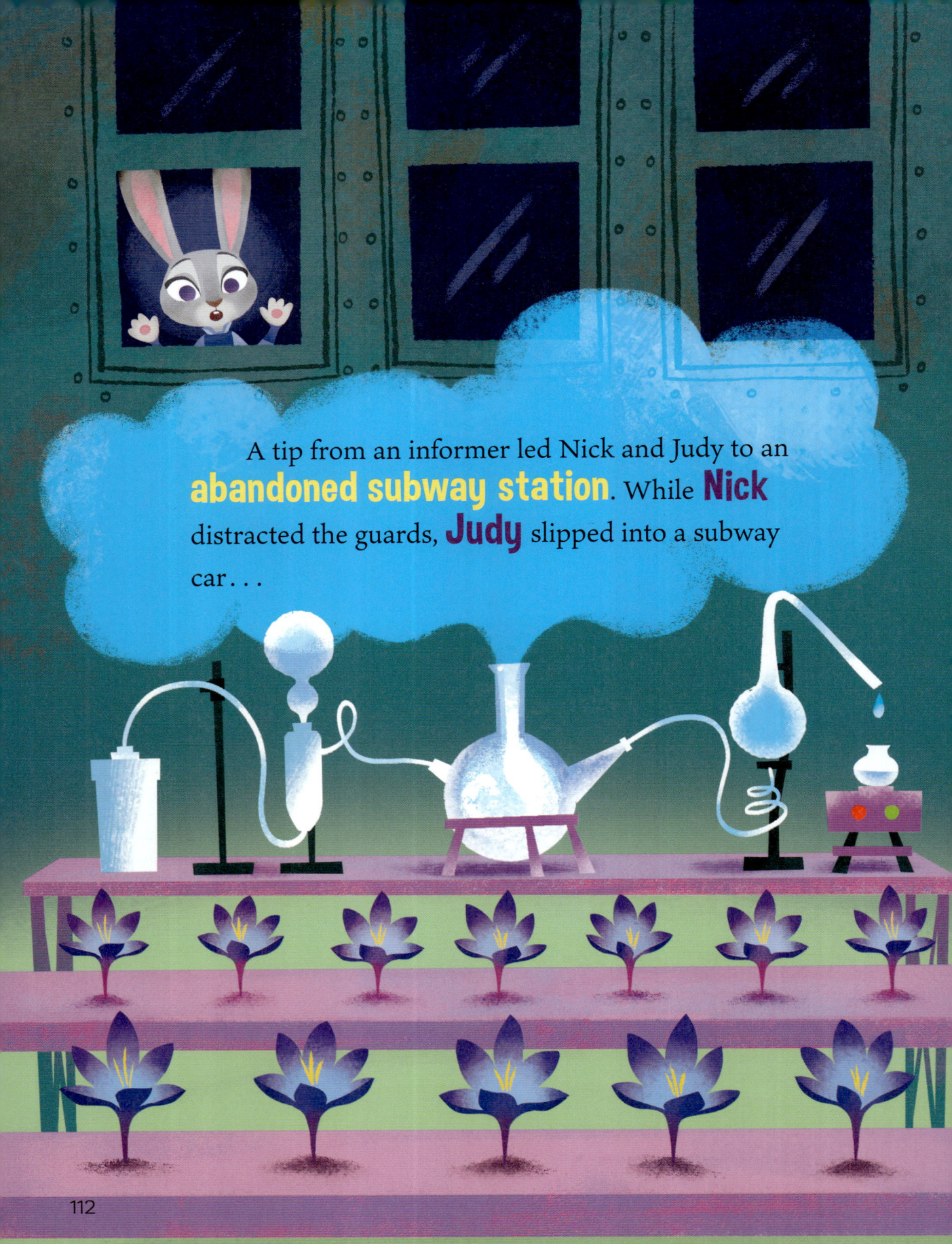

A tip from an informer led Nick and Judy to an **abandoned subway station**. While **Nick** distracted the guards, **Judy** slipped into a subway car...

. . . that was also a **secret laboratory**! Judy saw a ram create a **serum** using a flower. She learned that the serum caused mammals to turn **WILD**!

Nick and Judy grabbed the serum and ran . . . until they were cornered by **Assistant Mayor Bellwether**!

The sneaky sheep had created the serum because she knew that if animals with claws and fangs—**predators**—became savage, citizens would be scared of them. Then the smaller animals could lock them up and take over!

Bellwether shot a **dart** filled with the serum into Nick! The fox sank to all fours and started shaking. Bellwether **smiled**. She expected Nick to become savage and eat Judy!

But Nick **didn't** turn wild. He and Judy had pulled their greatest trick. They had **switched the serum** with **blueberry juice**!

Nick and Judy gave the evidence to **Chief Bogo**, and Bellwether was **arrested**.

All the animals who had gone savage—including Mr. Otterton—would soon be **cured**.

Judy and Nick had **solved the case**, and proved that they were far more than a dumb bunny and a sly fox. They were **partners**— and **best friends**—ready to fight crime in Zootopia!

Characters

Elsa

Anna

Christoff

Olaf

Sven

Key Words

- lullaby — 명 자장가
- imagination — 명 상상력
- discover — 동 발견하다
- mysterious — 형 신비한
- enormous — 형 거대한
- shot — shoot(쏘다)의 과거형, 과거분사
- blast — 명 폭발
- cliff — 명 절벽
- awaken — 동 깨다, 깨우다
- spirit — 명 영혼
- enchanted — 형 마법에 걸린
- nomadic — 형 유목의
- follow — 동 따라가다
- reveal — 동 드러내다
- similar — 형 비슷한
- mighty — 형 강력한, 힘센
- spread — 동 퍼지다, 확산되다
- reindeer — 명 순록
- flame — 명 불길, 불꽃
- calm — 동 진정시키다

Key Words

- [ ] feed — 동 먹이를 주다
- [ ] snowflake — 명 눈송이
- [ ] journey — 명 여행
- [ ] shipwreck — 명 난파선
- [ ] fear — 동 두려워하다
- [ ] rest — 명 나머지
- [ ] alone — 부 혼자
- [ ] form — 동 만들어 내다
- [ ] carry — 동 나르다
- [ ] protest — 동 항의하다
- [ ] accidentally — 부 우연히
- [ ] determined — 형 단호한, 확고한
- [ ] cross — 동 건너다, 가로지르다
- [ ] fierce — 형 격렬한
- [ ] equal — 형 동등한
- [ ] respect — 명 존경 동 존경하다
- [ ] sculpture — 명 조각상
- [ ] signal — 명 신호
- [ ] whisper — 명 속삭임
- [ ] restore — 동 회복시키다

Disney
FROZEN II

Adapted by
Nancy Cote

Illustrated by
Olga Mosqueda

Designed by
Tony Fejeran

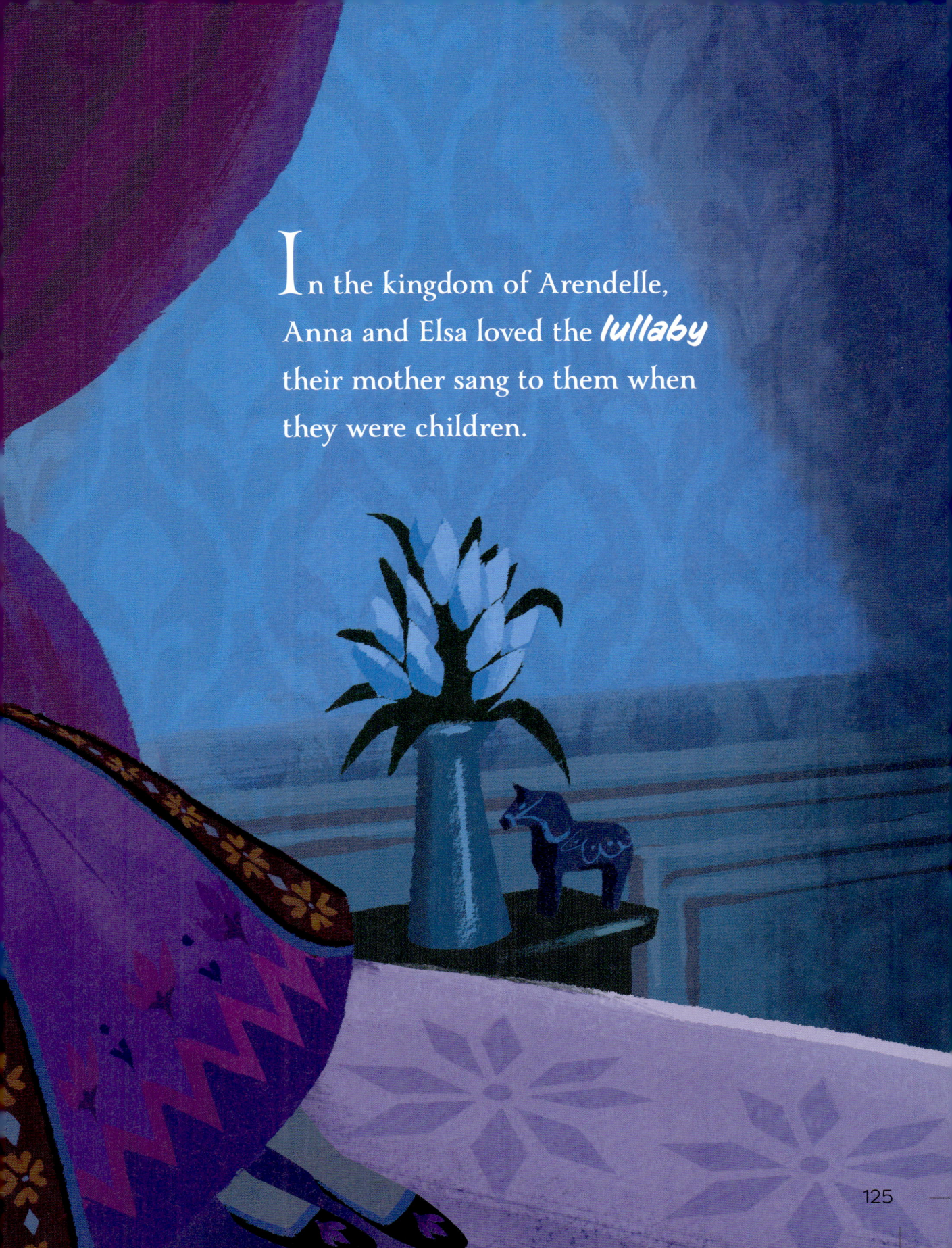

In the kingdom of Arendelle, Anna and Elsa loved the **lullaby** their mother sang to them when they were children.

The lullaby was about a **secret river**, which held all the answers about the past. It gave the girls a lot to think about and excited their *imaginations*.

As time went on, Anna and Elsa grew older. Elsa discovered her magical power over **snow and ice**, which became stronger and stronger. One night, a **mysterious voice** called to her. What did it want?

Elsa realized that the voice wanted her to travel north. She went to the fjord and shot out an enormous

icy blast!

It was clear that Elsa's magic had done something new and powerful.
But what did it mean?

The trolls rolled up to the cliffs to let Elsa know that her blast had awakened the spirits of the

Enchanted Forest.

They warned her that the spirits were *angry*. The forest was also where a nomadic group of people called the *Northuldra* were said to live.

Elsa knew in her heart that she must follow the mysterious voice to the Enchanted Forest.

Anna and her friends Kristoff, Olaf, and Sven went with Elsa. In the forest, they met the **Wind Spirit**, who whooshed around them.

They also met the Northuldra people, who told them **stories** and revealed that they were more **similar** to Elsa, Anna, and their friends than they were **different**.

While Elsa and her friends were getting to know the Northuldra, the mighty **Fire Spirit** appeared and set the Enchanted Forest on fire! Elsa tried to **stop** the spreading fire with her magic, but it wasn't working.

Kristoff **helped** Anna and the reindeer escape the flames.

Elsa was finally able to calm the Fire Spirit by feeding it **snowflakes**. The Fire Spirit was actually a little salamander.

Elsa heard the voice again, and she noticed that the Fire Spirit could hear it, too.

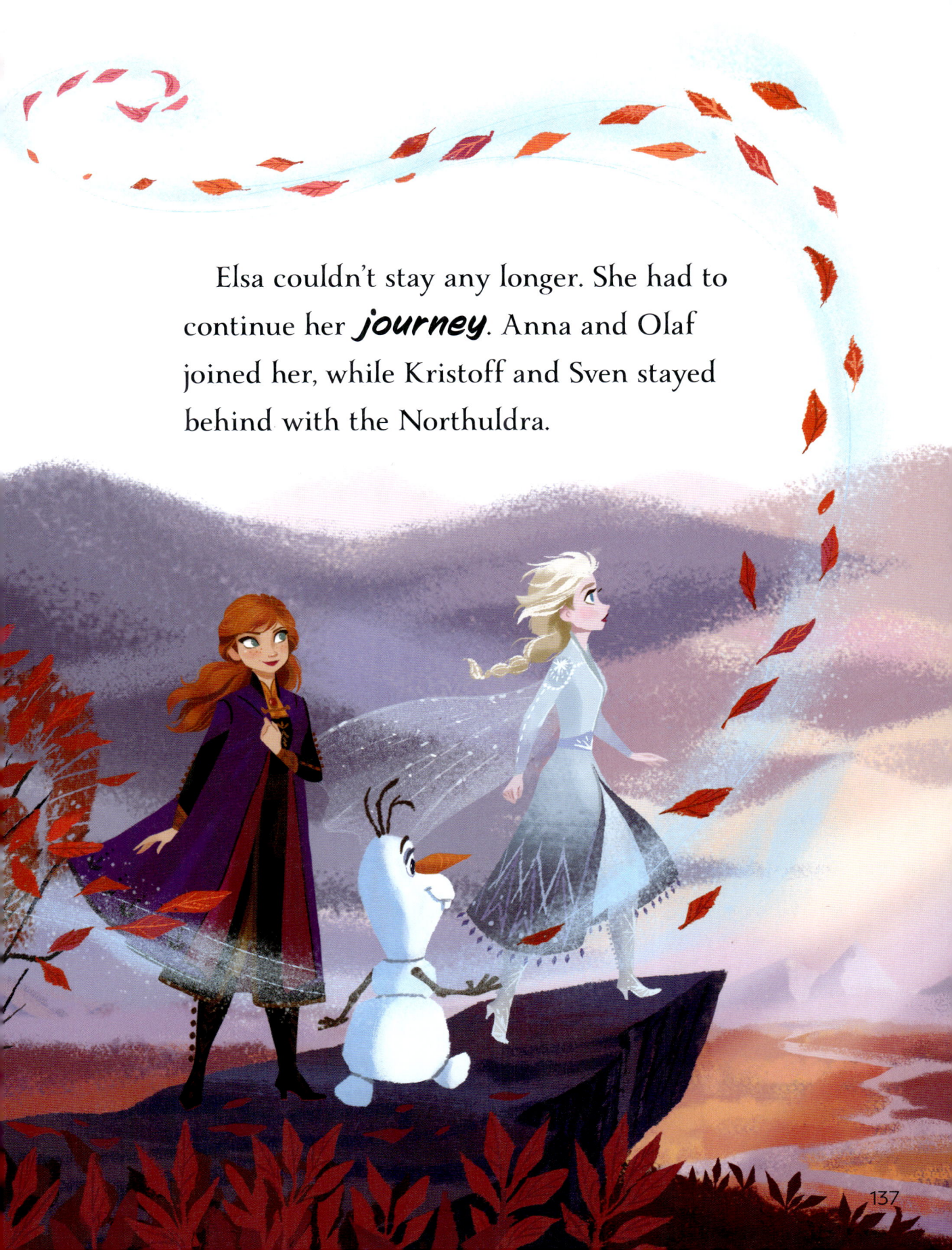

Elsa couldn't stay any longer. She had to continue her *journey*. Anna and Olaf joined her, while Kristoff and Sven stayed behind with the Northuldra.

Heading north, Anna and Elsa discovered their **parents' shipwreck**!

Inside the ship, they studied a map and learned that their parents had traveled north to understand why Elsa had magic.

Elsa feared losing Anna, just as she had lost their parents. Elsa decided to make the rest of the journey alone.

With a heavy heart, Elsa formed a boat made of ice that **scooped up** Anna and Olaf and carried them safely away.

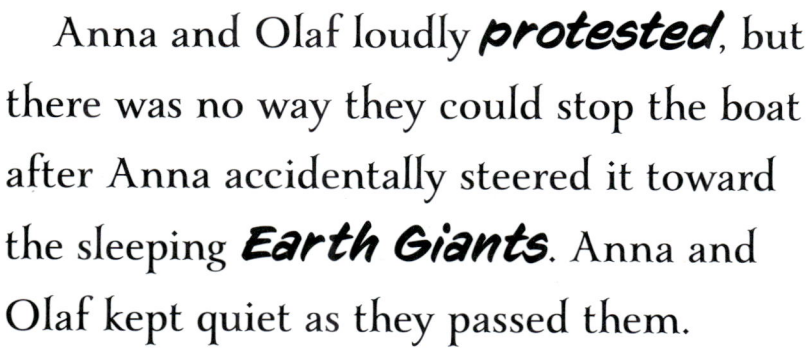

Anna and Olaf loudly **protested**, but there was no way they could stop the boat after Anna accidentally steered it toward the sleeping **Earth Giants**. Anna and Olaf kept quiet as they passed them.

More determined than ever, Elsa reached the next part of her journey: the **Dark Sea**. Now she needed to cross it.

The **Water Nokk** reared up from the sea and tried to stop Elsa. After a fierce battle, Elsa and the Water Nokk realized that their powers were equal. A mutual respect formed between them.

Meanwhile, Anna and Olaf's journey continued into a cave, where an **ice sculpture** appeared in front of them. It was a signal from Elsa. The journey had answered some of the queen's questions.

Elsa had **finally arrived** in the north! The voice that had called to her now quieted to a **whisper**, and she realized it had been within her all along. It had guided her to discover her inner peace.

By working together, the sisters were able to restore peace and harmony to the land at last.

Disney · PIXAR
Story Collection 3

Activity Book

Disney · Pixar Story Collection 3

Book Quiz

CONTENTS

Book Quiz

Moana	3
Coco	5
Incredibles 2	7
Zootopia	9
Frozen 2	11

Activities

Moana	13
Coco	21
Incredibles 2	29
Zootopia	37
Frozen 2	45
The Answers	53

★ 북 퀴즈
스토리를 읽고 나서 얼마나 정확히 이해했는지 북 퀴즈를 통해 이해도를 테스트합니다.
스토리의 중심 주제와 세부사항에 관한 문제로,
맞힌 개수에 따라 자신의 독해력을 확인할 수 있어요.

★ 학습 액티비티
어휘력과 독해력을 길러주는 다양한 문제 액티비티가 수록되었습니다.
또한 이야기 전반을 다시 이해하며 글의 구조를 정리하는 연습을 합니다.

BOOK QUIZ
Moana

Name: _____   Date: _____ / _____ / _____

1. What did Moana love even when she was little?

   ① the mountains
   ② the ocean
   ③ the valleys
   ④ the city

2. Moana loved listening to _____ stories.

   ① Grandpa Hula's
   ② Chief Tui's
   ③ Chief Ale's
   ④ Gramma Tala's

3. What did the demigod Maui steal from Te Fiti?

   ① her crown
   ② her necklace
   ③ her heart
   ④ her ring

4. Who believed that the ocean was dangerous?

   ① Moana   ② Gramma Tala
   ③ Chief Tui   ④ Coco

5. What did the ocean give Moana?

   ① a special gift
   ② a small coconut
   ③ a pretty flower
   ④ a goldfish

6. When Moana turned sixteen, Gramma Tala took her to a hidden _____.

   ① island   ② garden
   ③ boat   ④ cavern

7. Gramma Tala's last wish was for Moana to journey across the _____.

   ① village   ② mountain
   ③ ocean   ④ cave

8. Who did Moana meet on a faraway island?

① Chief Tui　② her ancestor
③ Te Fiti　　④ Maui

9. Maui stole Moana's _____.

① boat　　② treasure
③ food　　④ necklace

10. What was Maui looking for?

① his family
② his pet
③ his magic fishhook
④ his super boat

11. Who was Tamatoa?

① a lobster creature
② a shark
③ a crab monster
④ a dolphin

12. What did Maui teach Moana along the way?

① to wayfind　② to fish
③ to hunt　　④ to surf

13. What was the name of the Lava monster in Te Fiti?

① Te Bah　② Te Kā
③ Te Suh　④ Te Mi

14. What did Moana do to help Te Kā remember?

① She gave Te Kā the heart.
② She told Maui to hide.
③ She told Te Kā to sleep.
④ She prayed for Te Kā.

15. What did Maui transform into after saying goodbye to Moana?

① a hawk　② a whale
③ a lion　　④ a butterfly

Score: _____ / 15

- Score 11~15: 이야기를 읽고 세부 내용을 잘 파악하고 있어요.
- Score 6~10: 이야기의 전체적인 흐름을 대체로 잘 파악하고 있어요.
- Score 0~5: 단어 학습을 한 후, 이야기를 다시 한번 읽어 보세요.

BOOK QUIZ
Coco

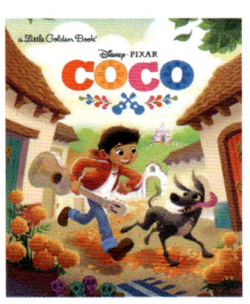

Name: _____   Date: _____ / _____ / _____

1. Where did Miguel Rivera live?

   ① in a small town   ② on a mountain
   ③ in the sea   ④ in a large city

2. Who was Mamá Coco?

   ① Miguel's sister
   ② Miguel's aunt
   ③ Miguel's cousin
   ④ Miguel's great-grandmother

3. What is Día de los Muertos?

   ① the Day of the Married
   ② the Day of the Dead
   ③ the Day of the Living
   ④ the Day of the Young

4. What was the one rule in the Rivera household?

   ① No books!   ② No TV!
   ③ No games!   ④ No music!

5. Ernesto de la Cruz is Miguel's favorite _____.

   ① soccer player
   ② actor
   ③ teacher
   ④ musician

6. What happened when Dante jumped onto the family ofrenda?

   ① Mamá Imelda's cup cracked.
   ② Mamá Imelda's photo crashed.
   ③ Mamá Imelda's plate dropped.
   ④ Mamá Imelda's candle broke.

7. Where was the famous guitar hung?

   ① in Miguel's house
   ② at Ernesto's tomb
   ③ in Mamá Coco's garden
   ④ in the church

8. What did Miguel notice when he gave Ernesto's guitar a strum?

① skeletons   ② ghosts
③ villagers   ④ animals

9. To return to the Land of the Living, Miguel needed a _____.

① gift   ② gold token
③ song   ④ blessing

10. Who did Miguel team up with to get a blessing?

① Mamá Imelda   ② Mamá Coco
③ Héctor   ④ Carlos

11. What would happen if Miguel didn't get Ernesto's blessing?

① He would turn into a fish.
② He would turn into a monster.
③ He would turn into a real skeleton.
④ He would turn into a horse.

12. What did Miguel do before falling into Ernesto's pool?

① He sang.   ② He cried.
③ He screamed. ④ He laughed.

13. Miguel discovered that Ernesto had _____ Héctor and stolen his songs.

① poisoned   ② trapped
③ ditched   ④ threw

14. The songs Héctor had written were all for his _____.

① friends   ② neighbors
③ family   ④ teachers

15. What song did Miguel sing to remind Mamá Coco of her papá?

① "Remember Me"
② "Help Me"
③ "Save Me"
④ "Pray for Me"

Score: _____ / 15

- Score 11~15: 이야기를 읽고 세부 내용을 잘 파악하고 있어요.
- Score 6~10: 이야기의 전체적인 흐름을 대체로 잘 파악하고 있어요.
- Score 0~5: 단어 학습을 한 후, 이야기를 다시 한번 읽어 보세요.

BOOK QUIZ
The Incredibles 2

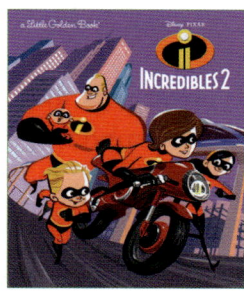

Name: _____   Date: _____ / _____ / _____

1. What started ripping up the city?

   ① a monster   ② a machine
   ③ a train   ④ a plane

2. What was Elastigirl's real name?

   ① Helen Parr   ② Violet Parr
   ③ Jasmin Parr ④ Selena Parr

3. Who was Winston Deavor?

   ① a doctor
   ② a famous singer
   ③ a wealthy businessman
   ④ a university student

4. Who got the first assignment to make Supers legal again?

   ① Mr. Incredible
   ② Dash
   ③ Elastigirl
   ④ Violet

5. Winston allowed Elastigirl's whole family to stay in one of his _____.

   ① ships   ② planes
   ③ hotels   ④ mansions

6. Which Incredible loved the mansion?

   ① Mr. Incredible   ② Dash
   ③ Violet   ④ Jack-Jack

7. What did Elastigirl spot on the first day at her new job?

   ① a runaway train
   ② a runaway bus
   ③ a runaway car
   ④ a runaway bicycle

8. Back at home, Bob was _____ from helping with homework, and changing diapers.

   ① exhausted   ② excited
   ③ nervous   ④ curious

9. Who was the super villain that took over an ambassador's helicopter?

   ① Green monster
   ② Screenslaver
   ③ Anteater
   ④ Beehiver

10. It turned out that _____ was the real Screenslaver.

    ① Evelyn Deavor
    ② Winston Deavor
    ③ Frozone
    ④ Jack-Jack

11. What did Evelyn put on Elastigirl to put her in a spell?

    ① a Hypno-mask
    ② Hypno-gloves
    ③ Hypno-goggles
    ④ a Hypno-hat

12. Bob needed help because Jack-Jack's powers were _____.

    ① interesting
    ② cool
    ③ amusing
    ④ uncontrollable

13. Who was captured by the group of hypnotized Supers?

    ① Frozone   ② Jack-Jack
    ③ Violet   ④ Dash

14. The Incredible kids appeared and _____ their parents and Frozone.

    ① attacked   ② hypnotized
    ③ freed   ④ captured

15. What happened in the end?

    ① The Supers were legal again.
    ② Frozone became an Incredible.
    ③ Violet went to school.
    ④ Elastigirl moved away.

Score: _____ / 15

- **Score 11~15:** 이야기를 읽고 세부 내용을 잘 파악하고 있어요.
- **Score 6~10:** 이야기의 전체적인 흐름을 대체로 잘 파악하고 있어요.
- **Score 0~5:** 단어 학습을 한 후, 이야기를 다시 한번 읽어 보세요.

BOOK QUIZ
Zootopia

Name: _____   Date: _____ / _____ / _____

1. Where did animals of all different sizes and shapes live happily?

   ① in the zoo   ② at school
   ③ in Zootopia   ④ in the library

2. What was Judy Hopps's job?

   ① a teacher   ② an artist
   ③ a doctor   ④ a police officer

3. What was Judy's first assignment?

   ① solving crimes
   ② singing songs
   ③ issuing parking tickets
   ④ hopping around

4. How many parking tickets did Judy write before lunchtime?

   ① only one ticket
   ② hundreds of tickets
   ③ thousands of tickets
   ④ no tickets

5. Where did Judy and Nick meet for the first time?

   ① in the office
   ② at a bus stop
   ③ at a cafe
   ④ in a classroom

6. What did a little fox want to eat?

   ① a sandwich   ② a Jumbo-pop
   ③ an apple   ④ a pawpsicle

7. Who did Nick and the little fox trick?

   ① Chief Bogo
   ② Judy
   ③ Mr. Otterton
   ④ Mayor Bellwether

8. How many days did Judy have to solve the crime?

   ① only one day   ② two days
   ③ three days   ④ a week

9. Who was missing?

① Nick
② Judy
③ Mr. Otterton
④ Bellwether

10. What did Judy use to record what Nick said?

① a phone
② a camera
③ a carrot pen
④ an umbrella

11. Judy and Nick helped each other to _____.

① find Mrs. Otterton's husband
② make the carrot pen
③ pay for an elephant-sized treat
④ go to Zootopia

12. The serum in the secret laboratory caused mammals to _____.

① turn happy
② turn sad
③ turn wild
④ turn hungry

13. What did Nick and Judy switch the serum with?

① carrot juice
② blueberry juice
③ pawpsicles
④ apple juice

14. At the end, Judy and Nick became _____.

① best partners
② worst friends
③ bad criminals
④ wild mammals

15. This story is about _____.

① equality
② peace
③ hope
④ love

Score: _____ / 15

- Score 11~15: 이야기를 읽고 세부 내용을 잘 파악하고 있어요.
- Score 6~10: 이야기의 전체적인 흐름을 대체로 잘 파악하고 있어요.
- Score 0~5: 단어 학습을 한 후, 이야기를 다시 한번 읽어 보세요.

BOOK QUIZ
Frozen 2

Name: _____   Date: _____ / _____ / _____

1. Who sang the lullaby that Elsa and Anna loved when they were children?

   ① their mother   ② their father
   ③ their aunt   ④ their uncle

2. What was the lullaby about?

   ① a secret forest
   ② a secret cave
   ③ a secret tree
   ④ a secret river

3. Elsa grew older and discovered her magical power over snow and _____.

   ① fire   ② flower
   ③ ice   ④ wind

4. In what direction did the voice want Elsa to travel?

   ① north   ② south
   ③ east   ④ west

5. Which spirits did Elsa awake with her blast?

   ① the Forbidden Mountain spirits
   ② the Enchanted Forest spirits
   ③ the Magical Ocean spirits
   ④ the Wind Valley spirits

6. What was the nomadic group of people called?

   ① the Hydra
   ② the Northuldra
   ③ the Ealandra
   ④ the Myastra

7. Who did Elsa, Anna, and their friends meet in the forest?

   ① the Land Spirit
   ② the Flower Spirit
   ③ the Water Spirit
   ④ the Wind Spirit

8. The mighty _____ Spirit appeared and set the Enchanted Forest on fire.

   ① Leaf   ② Moon
   ③ Sun   ④ Fire

9. What did Elsa feed the Fire Spirit to calm it down?

   ① ice cream   ② snowflakes
   ③ juice   ④ popsicles

10. Why did Elsa decide to make the rest of the journey alone?

    ① She didn't like to be with Anna.
    ② She missed her parents.
    ③ She feared losing Anna.
    ④ She was brave enough.

11. Anna accidentally steered the boat toward the sleeping _____ Giants.

    ① Earth   ② Sun
    ③ Moon   ④ Star

12. Which sea did Elsa need to cross to continue her journey?

    ① the Night Sea   ② the Dark Sea
    ③ the Yellow Sea   ④ the Bright Sea

13. Elsa and the Water _____ realized that their powers were equal.

    ① Nokk   ② Bear
    ③ Snake   ④ Stone

14. Where did Anna and Olaf see an ice sculpture?

    ① in a castle
    ② in the forest
    ③ in a cave
    ④ on a ship

15. The sisters were able to restore peace and _____ to the land.

    ① harmony
    ② joy
    ③ anger
    ④ sadness

Score: _____ / 15

- **Score 11~15:** 이야기를 읽고 세부 내용을 잘 파악하고 있어요.
- **Score 6~10:** 이야기의 전체적인 흐름을 대체로 잘 파악하고 있어요.
- **Score 0~5:** 단어 학습을 한 후, 이야기를 다시 한번 읽어 보세요.

Disney·Pixar Story Collection 3

Activities

WORD Check

A 다음 단어의 알맞은 우리말 뜻에 동그라미 하세요.

① drop (뻗치다 / 떨어뜨리다)
② wayfinder (길을 찾는 사람 / 상대)
③ fishhook (닻걸이 / 조각품)
④ current (해안 / 해류)
⑤ heart (심장 / 머리)
⑥ defeat (구하다 / 패배시키다)
⑦ faraway (가까운 / 멀리 떨어진)
⑧ gift (선수 / 선물)

B 빈칸에 알맞은 단어를 써 넣어 퍼즐을 완성하세요.

Across	① 폭풍우	② 금지하다	③ 대양, 바다
Down	④ 기대하다	⑤ 꽃을 피우다	⑥ 지도자, 리더

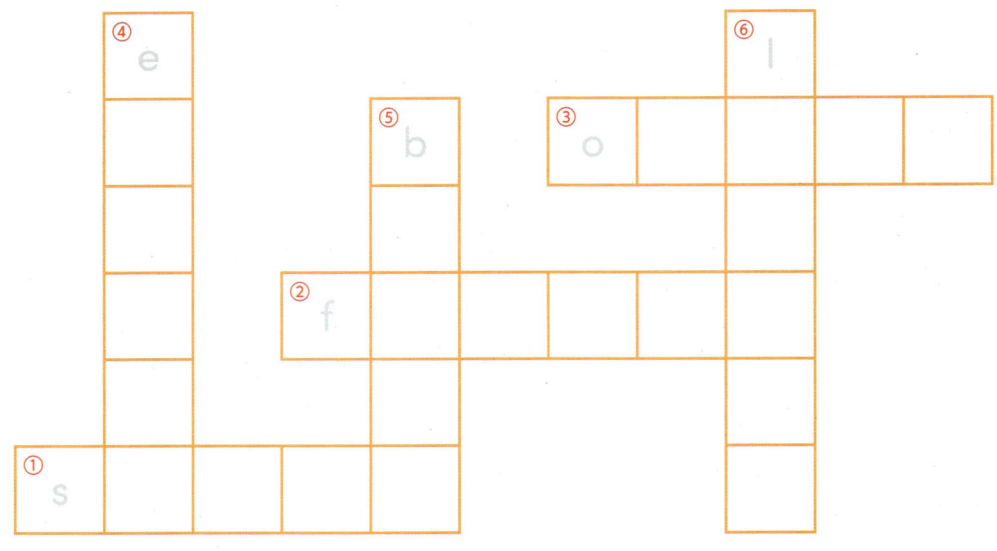

C 다음 단어를 사용하여 문장을 완성하세요.

| courage | ancient | retrieve |
| upset | transform | sail |

1. According to Gramma, Maui _____ the balance of nature by stealing the heart.

2. She led Moana to a hidden cavern full of _____ canoes.

3. With the heart safe inside her necklace, Moana set _____.

4. Thinking fast, Moana tricked Tamatoa, a crab monster, and she and Maui _____d the missing fishhook.

5. Summoning all her _____, Moana gave the heart to Te Kā.

6. Maui _____ed into a hawk and flew away.

STORY Check

A 모아나(Moana)의 주변 인물들에 대한 알맞은 설명을 찾아 써보세요.

Characters	What They Did
• Gramma Tala • Chief Tui • Maui	• He forbid the islanders to sail beyond the reef. • She told the story about Maui. • He stole the heart of the mother island.

1  Name: _____
What She Did: _____
_____
_____

2  Name: _____
What He Did: _____
_____
_____

3  Name: _____
What He Did: _____
_____
_____

B 각각의 장소에서 어떤 일이 일어났는지 맞게 연결해 보세요.

1. A hidden cavern — ⓐ — ⓓ Moana could feel the spirits of her ancestors.

2. The mother island, Te Fiti — ⓑ — ⓔ Moana tricked a crab monster, and she and Maui retrieved the missing fishhook.

3. Lalotai — ⓒ — ⓕ There was a lava monster named Te Kā!

C 다음 글에 알맞은 그림을 찾아 연결하세요.

1. Little Moana felt a deep connection to the ocean, and to all the creatures who belonged in it.

2. When Chief Tui picked up Moana, she dropped the gift.

3. Moana and her boat washed up on a faraway island, where she met Maui the demigod!

4. Moana and Maui had to get past the Kakamora, an army of wild, coconut-clad bandits.

5. Sailing on the open ocean was not easy for Moana — especially when a storm hit!

6. Moana and Maui said goodbye. Their journey together was complete.

SENTENCE Check

A 알맞은 단어에 동그라미 하여 문장을 완성하세요.

1. Moana also loved listening to Gramma Tala's [songs / stories].

2. The islanders were forbidden to [sail / look] beyond the reef!

3. When Chief Tui picked up Moana, she dropped the [gift / candy].

4. Gramma Tala believed the ocean's gift was the [heart / name] of Te Fiti!

5. So, with the heart [safe / broken] inside her necklace, Moana set sail.

6. But [fishing / sailing] on the open ocean was not easy for Moana.

7. When he tried to sail away, the [ocean / necklace] made sure Moana went with him.

8. Maui and Moana tried everything, but they could not [defeat / protect] Te Kā.

9. It was time for Moana to [retire / return] to her people.

10. The young [girl / princess] from Motunui now knew exactly who she was meant to be.

B 다음 단어들을 이용해 우리말 뜻에 맞는 문장을 완성하세요.

1 | of Motunui | the ocean | Moana | loved | . |

모투누이의 모아나는 바다를 사랑했어요.

→ _____

2 | a special gift | gave | Moana | the ocean | . |

바다는 모아나에게 특별한 선물을 주었어요.

→ _____

3 | boat | Maui | Moana's | stole | . |

마우이가 모아나의 보트를 훔쳤어요.

→ _____

4 | Te Kā | could not | they | defeat | . |

그들은 테카를 이길 수 없었어요.

→ _____

5 | in balance | the world | was back | . |

세상은 다시 균형을 되찾았어요.

→ _____

6 | their journey | complete | was | together | . |

그들이 함께 한 여행이 끝났어요.

→ _____

STORY MAP

문장의 빈칸을 채워 이야기의 구조를 한눈에 정리해 보세요.

| tricked | leader | balance | reached | return | restore |

Begining

Moana set sail to find Maui and ① _____ the heart of Te Fiti.

Middle

Maui promised to help ② _____ the heart of Te Fiti only if Moana helped him find his magic fishhook. Moana ③ _____ a crab monster, and Moana and Maui retrieved the missing fishhook.

Moana and Maui finally ④ _____ Te Fiti. But there was a lava monster named Te Kā. Moana gave the heart to Te Kā. And Te Kā remembered who she was meant to be.

Te Kā was Te Fiti! With her heart restored, Te Fiti bloomed once again.
The world was back in ⑤ _____.

End

Maui transformed into a hawk and flew away. Moana knew that she was a daughter, a ⑥ _____, and a wayfinder.

20

Disney·Pixar Story Collection 3

Activities

WORD Check

A 다음 단어의 알맞은 우리말 뜻에 동그라미 하세요.

1. ditch (버리다 / 공격하다)
2. discovery (폭발 / 발견)
3. full (가득한 / 감사하는)
4. poison (다투다 / 독살하다)
5. disappear (퍼지다 / 사라지다)
6. unidentified (정체불명의 / 비슷한)
7. relative (친척 / 친구)
8. blessing (축복 / 성공)

B 빈칸에 알맞은 단어를 써 넣어 퍼즐을 완성하세요.

Across	① 잊어버리다	② 굴러 떨어지다	③ 공연하다
Down	④ 사실, 진실	⑤ 붐비는	⑥ 구덩이

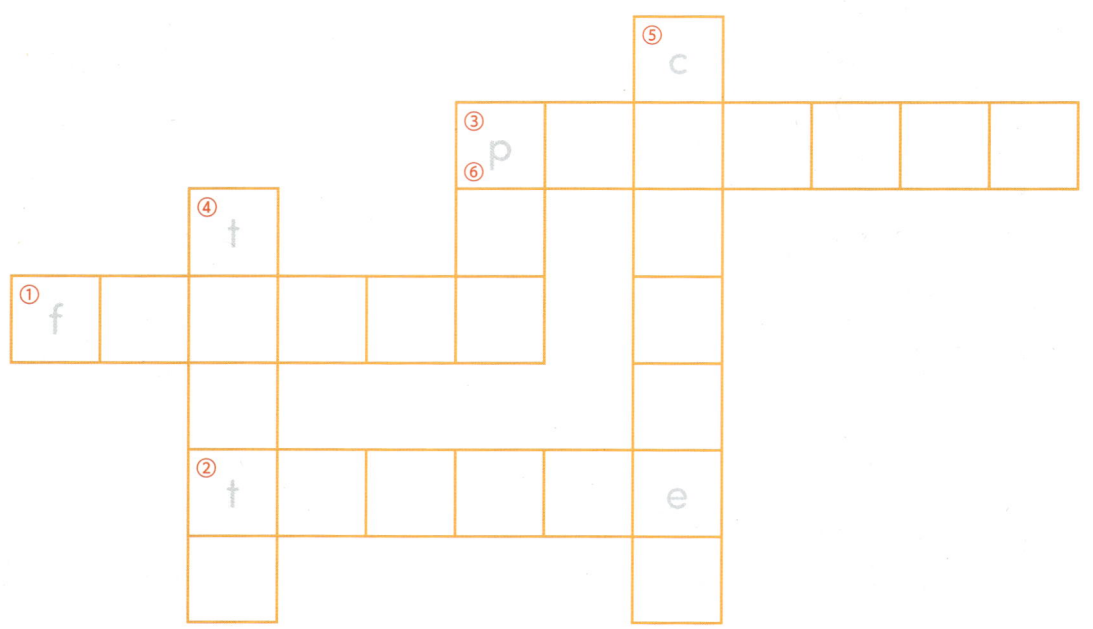

C 다음 단어를 사용하여 문장을 완성하세요.

| lullaby | memories | strum |
| support | overjoyed | remind |

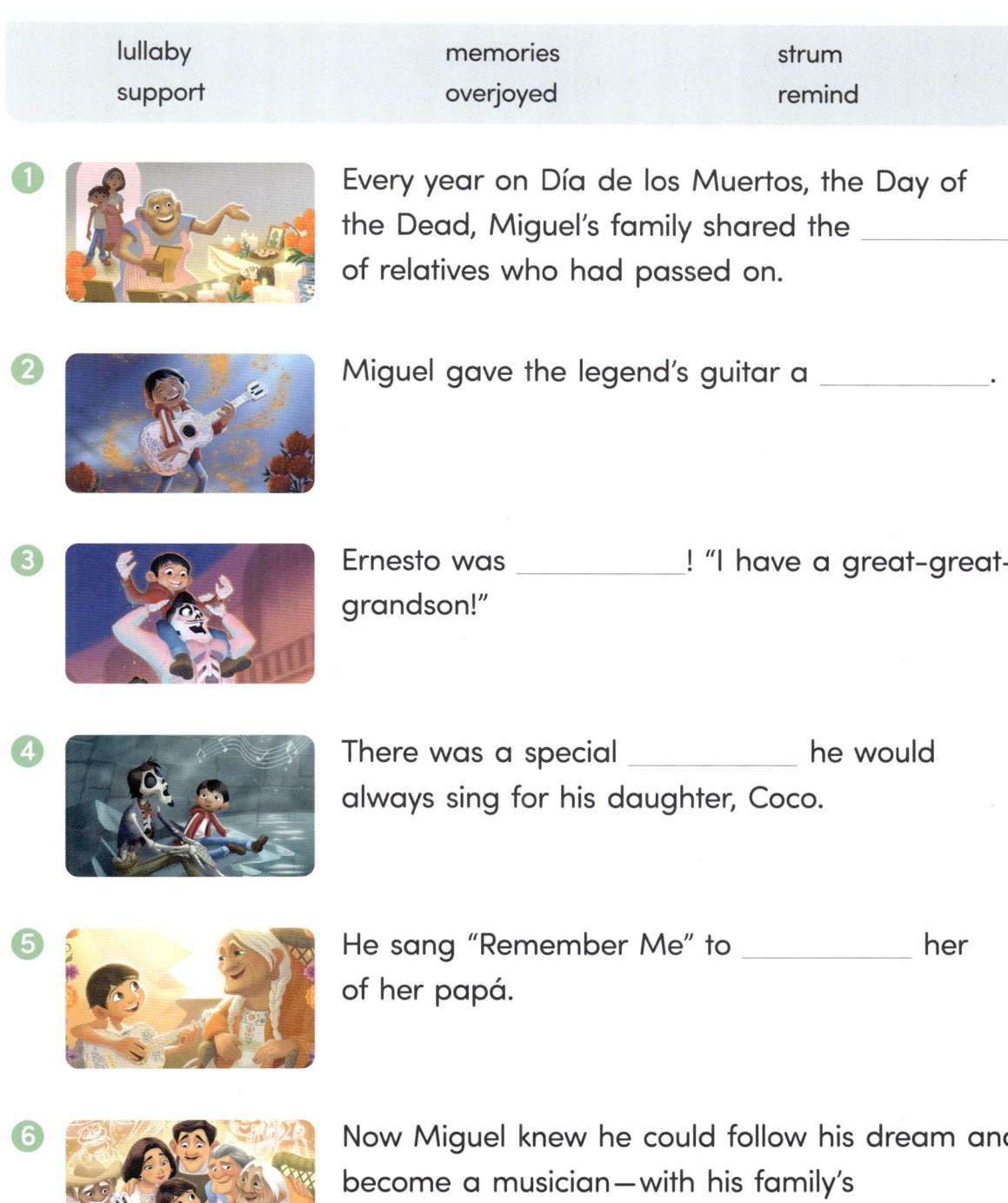

1. Every year on Día de los Muertos, the Day of the Dead, Miguel's family shared the _____ of relatives who had passed on.

2. Miguel gave the legend's guitar a _____.

3. Ernesto was _____! "I have a great-great-grandson!"

4. There was a special _____ he would always sing for his daughter, Coco.

5. He sang "Remember Me" to _____ her of her papá.

6. Now Miguel knew he could follow his dream and become a musician—with his family's _____.

STORY Check

A Miguel이 Ernesto의 기타를 가져간 원인과 그 결과를 정리해 보세요.

| destroyed | guitar | rule | heart |

[Cause]
Mamá Imelda's ① _____ had been broken by her musician husband.

[Effect 1]
There was one ② _____ in the Rivera household: No Music!

[Effect 2]
Miguel learned to play ③ _____ in his secret hideout.

[Effect 3]
Miguel's abuelita took his guitar and ④ _____ it.

B 이야기와 일치하는 문장에는 T, 일치하지 않는 문장에는 F에 동그라미 하세요.

1. Miguel and Imelda traveled all over looking for Héctor.   T F

2. Héctor began to disappear because his daughter was starting to forget him.   T F

3. Miguel learned that Ernesto had poisoned Héctor and stolen his photos to become famous.   T F

4. To return to the Land of the Living, Miguel would need a blessing from one of his dead family members.   T F

C 다음 글에 알맞은 그림을 찾아 연결하세요.

1. Mamá Imelda said she wouldn't give him her blessing if he wanted to be a musician.

2. "Mamá Coco's papa was Ernesto de la Cruz!" Miguel cried. "I'm going to be a musician!"

3. Héctor appeared, and as the two men argued, Miguel learned the dark truth.

4. They followed the path of marigold petals to visit their living relatives for Día de los Muertos.

5. If he didn't get Ernesto's blessing soon, he'd turn into a real skeleton and never get home!

6. They even performed together in a talent show!

SENTENCE Check

A 알맞은 단어에 동그라미 하여 문장을 완성하세요.

1. In the small [island / town] of Santa Cecilia, there lived a boy named Miguel Rivera.

2. In his secret hideout, he learned to play [piano / guitar] by watching videos of his favorite musician, Ernesto de la Cruz.

3. Because of their family [fiesta / rule], his abuelita took his guitar and destroyed it.

4. Miguel ran as fast as he could to Ernesto's [house / tomb], where the famous guitar still hung.

5. He and Dante crossed the Marigold Bridge into the Land of the [Dead / Living].

6. They even [performed / sat] together in a talent show!

7. Everyone watched as he sang and fell into Ernesto's [chair / pool].

8. Héctor appeared and as the two men argued, Miguel learned the [dark / funny] truth.

9. Then he threw Miguel and Héctor down into a dark [pit / cave].

10. Miguel knew he could follow his [friend / dream] and become a musician with his family's support.

B 다음 단어들을 이용해 우리말 뜻에 맞는 문장을 완성하세요.

1. | Miguel | but | music | loved | . |

하지만 미겔은 음악을 좋아했어요.

→ _____

2. | Mamá Imelda's | a guitar | was holding | husband | . |

마마 이멜다의 남편은 기타를 들고 있었어요.

→ _____

3. | to be | I need | this | like you | a musician | ! |

당신과 같은 음악가가 되기 위해 저는 이것이 필요해요!

→ _____

4. | traveled | all over | Ernesto | they | looking for | . |

그들은 에르네스토를 찾아 여기저기를 여행했어요.

→ _____

5. | a living boy | the skeletons | he was | saw that | . |

그가 살아 있는 소년인 것을 해골들이 보았어요.

→ _____

6. | Héctor | to disappear | but | began | . |

그러나 헥터는 사라지기 시작했어요.

→ _____

STORY MAP

문장의 빈칸을 채워 이야기의 구조를 한눈에 정리해 보세요.

| music | blessing | musician | disappear | remind | poisoned |

Background | Because of Mamá Imelda's ① _____ husband, there was one rule in the Rivera household: No Music!

Problem

When Miguel gave Ernesto's guitar a strum, he noticed all the skeletons.
Miguel needed a ② _____ from one of his dead family members to return to the Land of the Living.

Miguel met Ernesto at Ernesto's fiesta. But Miguel learned that Ernesto had ③ _____ Héctor and stolen his songs to become famous.

How the Problem Was Solved

Miguel found out Héctor was his great-great-grandpa. But Héctor began to ④ _____. His daughter was starting to forget him.
Mamá Imelda and Héctor sent Miguel home with their blessing.

Back in the Land of the Living, Miguel sang "Remember Me" to ⑤ _____ Mamá Coco of her papa.

Conclusion | The Riveras realized that ⑥ _____ could bring them closer together.

Disney · Pixar Story Collection 3

Activities

WORD Check

A 다음 단어의 알맞은 우리말 뜻에 동그라미 하세요.

① exhausted   (지쳐버린 / 신나는)
② stretch   (움츠리다 / 뻗다)
③ zoom   (머무르다 / 쌩 하고 가다)
④ attack   (공격하다 / 반대하다)
⑤ uncontrollable   (통제할 수 없는 / 무서운)
⑥ assignment   (충돌 / 임무)
⑦ undercover   (비밀리에 하는 / 대표로 하는)
⑧ opponent   (리더 / 상대)

B 빈칸에 알맞은 단어를 써 넣어 퍼즐을 완성하세요.

Across	① 못된, 사악한	② 사로잡다	③ 고마워하는
Down	④ 합법적인	⑤ 구하다	⑥ 풀어 주다

C. 다음 단어를 사용하여 문장을 완성하세요.

| villain | stretch | challenge |
| criminal | fierce | pounce |

1.  She _____ed into a parachute and slowed down the train.

2.  It was an intruder! Jack-Jack tried to stop the _____.

3.  During her first TV interview, a super _____ called the Screenslaver attacked.

4.  When Mr. Incredible arrived at the Deavors' ship, a hypnotized Elastigirl _____d on him!

5.  Evelyn was a _____ opponent, but she was no match for Elastigirl.

6.  Now the Incredibles were ready to face any _____—as a family!

STORY Check

A 수퍼 패밀리(Family of Supers)에게 일어난 문제들이 어떻게 해결되었는지 맞게 연결해 보세요.

Problem

1. Bob needed some serious help with Jack-Jack. The baby's powers were uncontrollable!

2. Everyone on board was under Evelyn's wicked spell.

3. A group of hypnotized Supers arrived to capture the kids.

Solution

a. Suddenly, the kids appeared. They freed their parents and Frozone from the hypnosis.

b. Edna made a special supersuit and tracker to help manage Jack-Jack's powers.

c. Frozone showed up just in time to help.

B 아래 등장인물에 해당하는 문장을 찾아 기호를 쓰세요.

ⓐ A wealthy businessman proposed a plan to make Supers legal again.
ⓑ She was the real Screenslaver! She wanted to destroy her brother's plan and make sure Supers were never legal again.
ⓒ The Incredibles' friend joined in the fight.

1  ☐

2  ☐

3  ☐

C 다음 글에 알맞은 그림을 찾아 연결하세요.

1. When a machine started ripping up the city, the Incredibles sprang into action!

2. Dash used a remote control to move the floors and turn on the waterfalls.

3. Elastigirl hopped onto her Elasticycle and chased the train through the city.

4. Bob heard the commotion and ran outside. He couldn't believe his eyes. "You... have... Powers!"

5. The Incredibles and Frozone battled the rest of the hypnotized Supers.

6. She scrambled over rooftops, zoomed up a crane, and zipped through a tunnel.

SENTENCE Check

A 알맞은 단어에 동그라미 하여 문장을 완성하세요.

1. The Incredibles stopped the machine but got in big [sorrow / trouble].

2. Elastigirl was nervous, but this was her [chance / change] to help her family and all Supers.

3. On Elastigirl's first day at her new job, she spotted a runaway [horse / train].

4. Helping with homework, changing [sheets / diapers], and dealing with teenage drama really knocked him out.

5. The next day, the city buzzed with the news of Elastigirl's amazing [recovery / rescue].

6. Elastigirl realized she'd caught the wrong [vehicle / person].

7. The baby's [words / powers] were uncontrollable!

8. Bob asked Frozone to [ask / watch] the kids and then rushed away.

9. Violet flung razor-sharp force fields at the Super until she and Dash could [rest / escape].

10. Now the Incredibles were ready to [fight / face] any challenge as a family!

B 다음 단어들을 이용해 우리말 뜻에 맞는 문장을 완성하세요.

1. | was exhausted | at home, | Bob | back | . |

   집에 돌아와서, 밥은 녹초가 되었어요.
   → _____

2. | under | she | was | Evelyn's spell | . |

   그녀는 에블린의 마법에 걸렸어요.
   → _____

3. | were | uncontrollable | the baby's | powers | . |

   아기의 힘은 통제할 수 없었어요.
   → _____

4. | Jack-Jack | to the smartest | Bob brought | person he knew | . |

   밥은 그가 아는 가장 똑똑한 사람에게 잭잭을 데려갔어요.
   → _____

5. | was ready | together | the family | to fight | ! |

   가족들은 함께 싸울 준비가 되었어요!
   → _____

6. | to the Supers | grateful | was | everyone | . |

   모두가 슈퍼 히어로들에게 고마워했어요.
   → _____

STORY MAP

문장의 빈칸을 채워 이야기의 흐름을 한눈에 정리해 보세요.

| freed | stopped | rescued | spell | capture | eyes | forced | lost |

 Elastigirl ① _____ the ambassador from the Screenslaver. And she captured him.

 Evelyn Deavor, the real Screenslaver, put hypno-goggles on Elastigirl. Then she was under Evelyn's ② _____.

 A group of hypnotized Supers arrived to ④ _____ the kids. The amazing Incredible whisked the kids away.

 Mr. Incredible arrived at Deavor's ship. Elastigirl put hypno-goggles over his ③ _____.

 The Incredible brought the kids to the ship. Dash and Violet tracked their ⑤ _____ brother.

 Evelyn ⑥ _____ the Supers to set the ship on a crash course toward the city.

 All the Supers turned the ship around and ⑧ _____ it just before it reached the shore.

 The kids ⑦ _____ their parents and Frozone from the hypnosis.

Disney · Pixar Story Collection 3

Disney
ZOOTOPIA
Activities

WORD Check

A 다음 단어의 알맞은 우리말 뜻에 동그라미 하세요.

1. otter (수달 / 숫양)
2. clue (발톱 / 단서)
3. achieve (실망하다 / 성취하다)
4. wild (놀라운 / 야생의)
5. sneaky (순수한 / 교활한)
6. arrest (체포하다 / 발견하다)
7. prove (증명하다 / 잠입하다)
8. case (사건 / 동굴)

B 빈칸에 알맞은 단어를 써 넣어 퍼즐을 완성하세요.

Across	① 범죄	② 증거	③ 모양
Down	④ 속임수	⑤ 만료된, 기한이 지난	⑥ 발톱

C 다음 단어를 사용하여 문장을 완성하세요.

| equal | solve | resold |
| record | switch | assignment |

1.  Everyone was _____, whether they had long claws or little paws.

2.  Judy hopped with excitement as she waited for her first _____.

3.  Judy wanted to _____ crimes, not be a meter maid.

4.  Nick melted the Jumbo-pop and _____ pawpsicles for a big profit!

5.  She used her carrot pen to _____ him talking about his shady business deals!

6.  Judy and Nick had _____ed the serum with blueberry juice!

STORY Check

A 등장인물들에 대한 알맞은 설명을 찾아 기호를 쓰세요.

ⓐ She was the first bunny ever to join the Zootopia Police Department.	ⓑ She shot a dart filled with the serum into Nick!	ⓒ He melted the Jumbo-pop to create smaller pawpsicles.
ⓓ She wanted to solve crimes, not be a meter maid.	ⓔ He resold pawpsicles for a big profit.	ⓕ She expected Nick to become savage and eat Judy.

❶ Nick 　☐ , ☐

❷ Judy 　☐ , ☐

❸ Bellwether 　☐ , ☐

B 벨웨더 부시장이 나쁜 일을 저지른 이유를 정리해 보세요.

[Effect]

 Assistant Mayor Bellweather ① _____ the serum.

lock
scared
created

[Cause 1]

She knew that if animals with claws and fangs — predators — became savage, citizens would be ② _____ of them.

[Cause 2]

She thought the smaller animals could ③ _____ up the predators and take over the city!

C 다음 글에 알맞은 그림을 찾아 연결하세요.

1. Animals of all different sizes and shapes lived and worked together happily.

2. There she met a little fox who was desperate for a Jumbo-pop.

3. Judy wrote hundreds of parking tickets before lunchtime.

4. Judy got her chance. Mrs. Otterton's husband was missing, and Judy offered to take the case.

5. Nick and Judy worked together and escaped. They were becoming friends.

6. Nick and Judy grabbed the serum and ran until they were cornered by Assistant Mayor Bellwether!

SENTENCE Check

A 알맞은 단어에 동그라미 하여 문장을 완성하세요.

1. Everyone was equal, whether they had long claws or little [paws / tails].

2. Judy hopped with excitement as she waited for her first [assignment / crime].

3. His dad, Nick, was out of cash, so Judy offered to [play / pay].

4. But Judy had only two days to solve the [crime / quiz].

5. The [answer / plan] was to question Mr. Manchas, the last animal to have seen the otter.

6. Nick and Judy found Mr. Manchas, but something was [new / wrong] with him.

7. Using security camera footage, she led Nick to a scary building on the edge of [street / town].

8. Judy learned that the serum caused mammals to [die / turn] wild.

9. Bellwether expected Nick to [become / look] savage and eat Judy!

10. They were [opposites / partners] and best friends ready to fight crime in Zootopia!

B 다음 단어들을 이용해 우리말 뜻에 맞는 문장을 완성하세요.

1 | anything | can | be | anyone | ! |

누구나 무엇이든 될 수 있어요!

→ _____

2 | wanted | a good job | to do | Judy | . |

주디는 일을 잘 하고 싶었어요.

→ _____

3 | Judy | that night, | disappointed | went to bed | . |

그날 밤, 주디는 실망한 채로 잠자리에 들었어요.

→ _____

4 | had | Judy | to solve the crime | only two days | . |

주디는 사건을 해결하는 데 겨우 이틀의 시간이 주어졌어요.

→ _____

5 | becoming | they | friends | were | . |

그들은 친구가 되어가고 있었어요.

→ _____

6 | didn't turn | but | wild | Nick | . |

그러나 닉은 야생 동물로 변하지 않았어요.

→ _____

STORY MAP

문장의 빈칸을 채워 이야기의 구조를 한눈에 정리해 보세요.

| shot | arrested | serum | wild | building | missing |

Judy's First Case

Mrs. Otterton's husband was ① _____.

How the Crime Was Solved

Nick and Judy found Mr. Manchas. He was the last animal to have seen the otter. But he had gone ② _____.

Using security camera footage, Judy led Nick to a scary ③ _____ on the edge of town. Inside, they found more wild-eyed animals—including the missing otter.

Nick and Judy found a secret laboratory in the abandoned subway station.
Judy saw a ram create a ④ _____ using a flower.
She learned that the serum caused mammals to turn wild.

Bellwether ⑤ _____ a dart filled with the serum into Nick. But Nick and Judy had switched the serum with blueberry juice.

Nick and Judy gave the evidence to Chief Bogo, and Bellwether was ⑥ _____.

Disney·Pixar Story Collection 3

Disney
FROZEN II

Activities

WORD Check

A 다음 단어의 알맞은 우리말 뜻에 동그라미 하세요.

① mysterious (신비한 / 즐거운) ② similar (다른 / 비슷한)

③ spread (사라지다 / 퍼지다) ④ protest (동의하다 / 항의하다)

⑤ sculpture (골동품 / 조각품) ⑥ mighty (강력한 / 완벽한)

⑦ lullaby (자장가 / 아지트) ⑧ determined (포기한 / 단호한)

B 빈칸에 알맞은 단어를 써 넣어 퍼즐을 완성하세요.

Across	① 여행	② 마법에 걸린	③ 폭발
Down	④ 혼자	⑤ 속삭임	⑥ 동등한

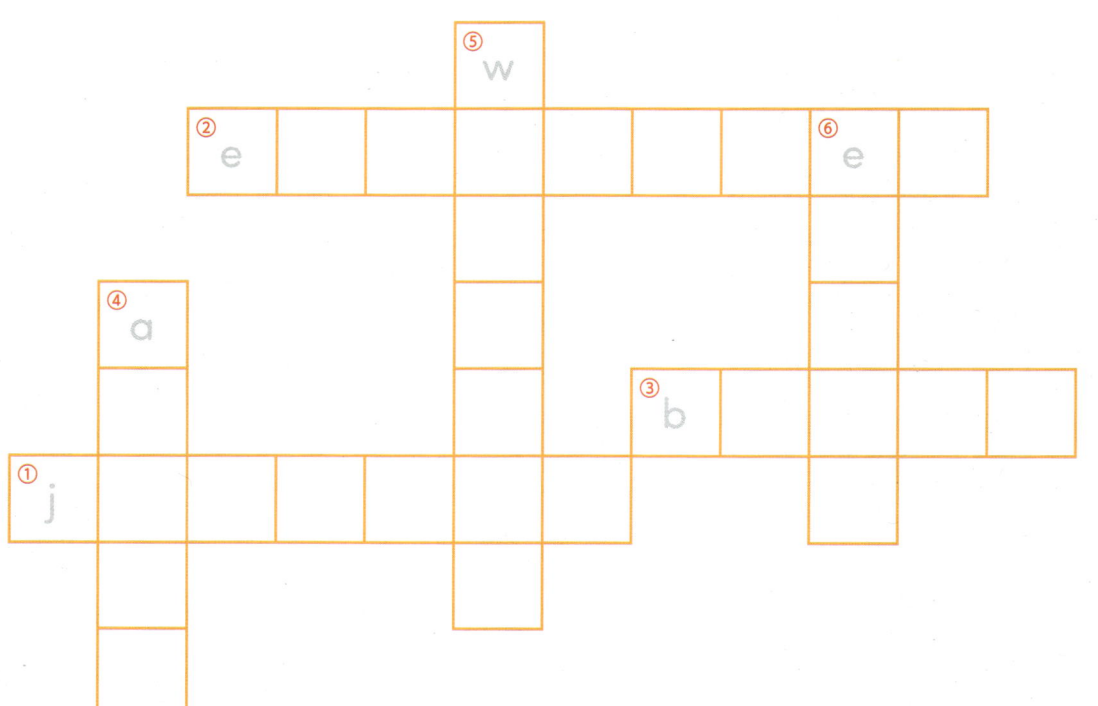

C 다음 단어를 사용하여 문장을 완성하세요.

| enormous | restore | cross |
| imaginations | shipwreck | snowflakes |

1. The lullaby gave the girls a lot to think about and excited their _____.

2. She went to the fjord and shot out an _____ icy blast.

3. Elsa reached the next part of her journey: the Dark Sea. Now she needed to _____ it.

4. Elsa was finally able to calm the Fire Spirit by feeding it _____.

5. Heading north, Anna and Elsa discovered their parents' _____!

6. By working together, the sisters were able to _____ peace and harmony to the land at last.

Frozen 2 47

STORY Check

A 다음 일들의 결과를 찾아 맞게 연결해 보세요.

Cause

1. Elsa feared losing Anna, just as she had lost their parents.
2. Elsa and the Water Nokk realized that their powers were equal.
3. Elsa's icy blast awakened the spirits of the Enchanted Forest.

Effect

ⓐ The trolls warned Elsa that the spirits were angry.

ⓑ Elsa decided to make the rest of the journey alone.

ⓒ A mutual respect formed between them.

B Elsa와 Anna가 여행을 하는 동안 일어났던 일들의 순서에 맞게 기호를 쓰세요.

ⓐ In the forest, they met the Wind Spirit, who whooshed around them.
ⓑ The Water Nokk reared up from the sea and tried to stop Elsa.
ⓒ They also met the Northuldra people.
ⓓ The mighty Fire Spirit appeared and set the Enchanted Forest on fire!

C 다음 글에 알맞은 그림을 찾아 연결하세요.

1. One night, a mysterious voice called to Elsa. What did it want?

2. The trolls rolled up to the cliffs to let Elsa know that her blast had awakened the spirits of the Enchanted Forest.

3. Anna and Olaf kept quiet as they passed the sleeping Earth Giants.

4. Inside the ship, they studied a map and learned that their parents had traveled north to understand why Elsa had magic.

5. Elsa formed a boat made of ice that scooped up Anna and Olaf and carried them safely away.

6. Anna and Olaf's journey continued into a cave, where an ice sculpture appeared in front of them.

SENTENCE Check

A 알맞은 단어에 동그라미 하여 문장을 완성하세요.

1. Elsa discovered her [magical / lost] power over snow and ice, which became stronger and stronger.

2. The trolls warned her that the spirits were [angry / hungry].

3. Elsa tried to stop the spreading fire with her magic, but it wasn't [moving / working].

4. Elsa was finally able to calm the Fire Spirit by [feeding / showing] it snowflakes.

5. Elsa heard the [news / voice] again, and she noticed that the Fire Spirit could hear it, too.

6. Heading north, Anna and Elsa discovered their parents' [kingdom / shipwreck]!

7. Elsa [feared / dreamed] losing Anna, just as she had lost their parents.

8. The Water Nokk reared up from the sea and tried to [stop / kill] Elsa.

9. The journey had answered some of the queen's [questions / wishes].

10. The voice had guided her to discover her inner [peace / magic].

B 다음 단어들을 이용해 우리말 뜻에 맞는 문장을 완성하세요.

① | a secret river | the lullaby | about | was | . |

그 자장가는 비밀의 강에 관한 것이었어요.

→ _____

② | them | the flames | escape | Kristoff helped | . |

크리스토프는 그들이 불길에서 탈출하도록 도왔어요.

→ _____

③ | discovered | their parents' | shipwreck | Anna and Elsa | ! |

안나와 엘사는 부모님의 난파선을 발견했어요!

→ _____

④ | any longer | couldn't | stay | Elsa | . |

엘사는 더 이상 머물 수 없었어요.

→ _____

⑤ | between them | a mutual respect | formed | . |

그들 사이에 서로의 존경이 형성되었어요.

→ _____

⑥ | a signal | it | from Elsa | was | . |

그것은 엘사의 신호였어요.

→ _____

STORY MAP

문장의 빈칸을 채워 이야기의 구조를 한눈에 정리해 보세요.

| voice | signal | peace | equal | shipwreck | follow |

Beginning

Elsa, Anna, and Anna's friends started to ① _____ the mysterious voice to the Enchanted Forest.

Middle

Heading north, Anna and Elsa discovered their parents' ② _____. Elsa feared losing Anna, so she decided to make the rest of the journey alone.

Elsa reached the Dark Sea. Then the Water Nokk reared up from the sea and tried to stop Elsa. But Elsa and Nokk realized that their powers were ③ _____. A mutual respect formed between them.

Anna and Olaf continued their journey. An ice sculpture appeared in front of them in the cave. It was a ④ _____ from Elsa.

End

Elsa finally arrived in the north! She realized the ⑤ _____ had been within her all along. At last, the sisters were able to restore ⑥ _____ and harmony to the land.

52

Disney · Pixar Story Collection 3

The Answers

BOOK QUIZ

Moana Book Quiz — p.3

1. ②   2. ④   3. ③   4. ③   5. ①   6. ④
7. ③   8. ④   9. ①   10. ③   11. ③   12. ①
13. ②   14. ①   15. ①

Coco Book Quiz — p.5

1. ①   2. ④   3. ②   4. ④   5. ④   6. ②
7. ②   8. ①   9. ④   10. ③   11. ③   12. ①
13. ①   14. ③   15. ①

The Incredibles 2 Book Quiz — p.7

1. ②   2. ①   3. ③   4. ③   5. ④   6. ②
7. ①   8. ①   9. ②   10. ①   11. ③   12. ④
13. ①   14. ③   15. ①

Zootopia Book Quiz — p.9

1. ③   2. ④   3. ③   4. ②   5. ③   6. ②
7. ②   8. ②   9. ③   10. ③   11. ①   12. ③
13. ②   14. ①   15. ①

Frozen 2 Book Quiz — p.11

1. ①   2. ④   3. ③   4. ①   5. ②   6. ②
7. ④   8. ④   9. ②   10. ③   11. ①   12. ②
13. ①   14. ③   15. ①

MOANA Activities

WORD Check — p.14

A
1. 떨어뜨리다
2. 길을 찾는 사람
3. 닻걸이
4. 해류
5. 심장
6. 패배시키다
7. 멀리 떨어진
8. 선물

B

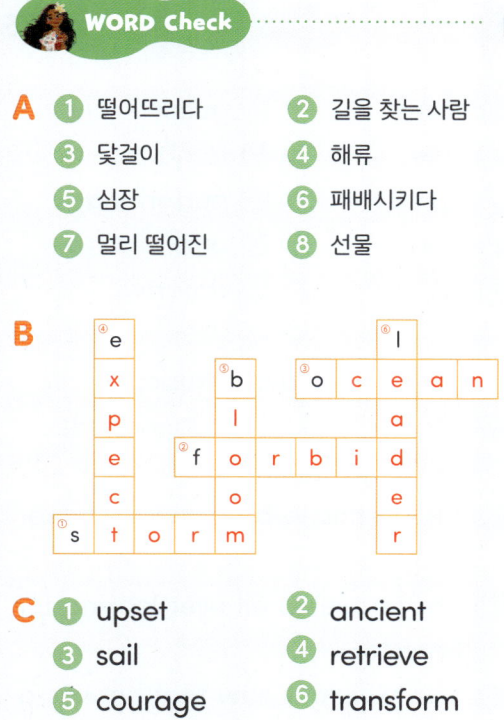

C
1. upset
2. ancient
3. sail
4. retrieve
5. courage
6. transform

SENTENCE Check — p.18

A
1. stories
2. sail
3. gift
4. heart
5. safe
6. sailing
7. ocean
8. defeat
9. return
10. girl

B
1. Moana of Motunui loved the ocean.
2. The ocean gave Moana a special gift.
3. Maui stole Moana's boat.
4. They could not defeat Te Kā.
5. The world was back in balance.
6. Their journey together was complete.

STORY Check — p.16

A
1. Gramma Tala — She told the story about Maui.
2. Maui — He stole the heart of the mother island.
3. Chief Tui — He forbid the islanders to sail beyond the reef.

B
1. ⓑ–ⓓ
2. ⓐ–ⓕ
3. ⓒ–ⓔ

C
1. ⓒ
2. ⓑ
3. ⓐ
4. ⓔ
5. ⓕ
6. ⓓ

STORY MAP — p.20

1. restore
2. return
3. tricked
4. reached
5. balance
6. leader

The Answers 55

COCO Activities

WORD Check — p.22

A
1. 버리다
2. 발견
3. 가득한
4. 독살하다
5. 사라지다
6. 정체불명의
7. 친척
8. 축복

B

Crossword:
- ① forget
- ② tooth (t u t h vertical... t/u/t/h)
- ③ perform
- ④ tiow...
- ⑤ crowded
- ⑥ tumbled

C
1. memories
2. strum
3. overjoyed
4. lullaby
5. remind
6. support

SENTENCE Check — p.26

A
1. town
2. guitar
3. rule
4. tomb
5. Dead
6. performed
7. pool
8. dark
9. pit
10. dream

B
1. But Miguel loved music.
2. Mamá Imelda's husband was holding a guitar.
3. I need this to be a musician like you!
4. They traveled all over looking for Ernesto.
5. The skeletons saw that he was a living boy.
6. But Héctor began to disappear.

STORY Check — p.24

A
1. heart
2. rule
3. guitar
4. destroyed

B
1. F   2. T   3. F   4. T

C
1. ⓒ
2. ⓓ
3. ⓑ
4. ⓕ
5. ⓐ
6. ⓔ

STORY MAP — p.28

1. musician
2. blessing
3. poisoned
4. disappear
5. remind
6. music

THE INCREDIBLES 2 Activities

WORD Check — p.30

A
① 지쳐버린 ② 뻗다
③ 쌩 하고 가다 ④ 공격하다
⑤ 통제할 수 없는 ⑥ 임무
⑦ 비밀리에 하는 ⑧ 상대

B
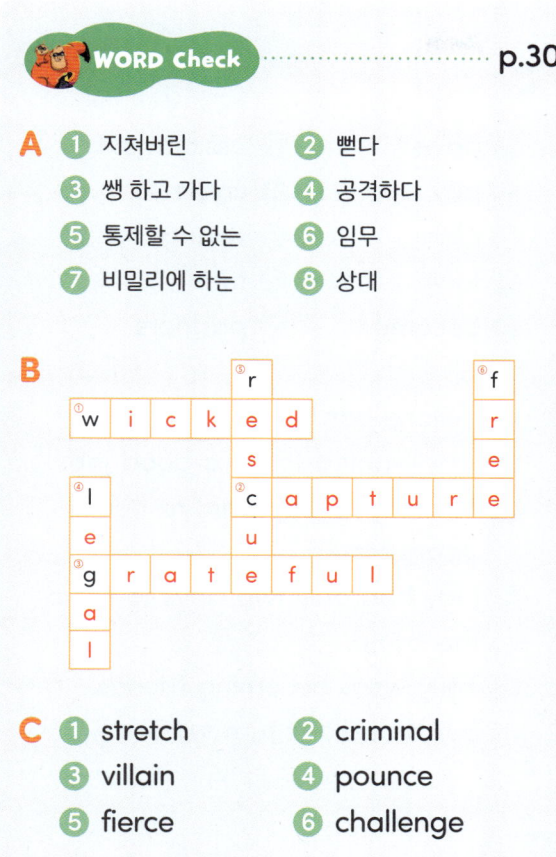

C
① stretch ② criminal
③ villain ④ pounce
⑤ fierce ⑥ challenge

SENTENCE Check — p.34

A
① trouble ② chance
③ train ④ diapers
⑤ rescue ⑥ person
⑦ powers ⑧ watch
⑨ escape ⑩ face

B
① Back at home, Bob was exhausted.
② She was under Evelyn's spell.
③ The baby's powers were uncontrollable.
④ Bob brought Jack-Jack to the smartest person he knew.
⑤ The family was ready to fight together!
⑥ Everyone was grateful to the Supers.

STORY Check — p.32

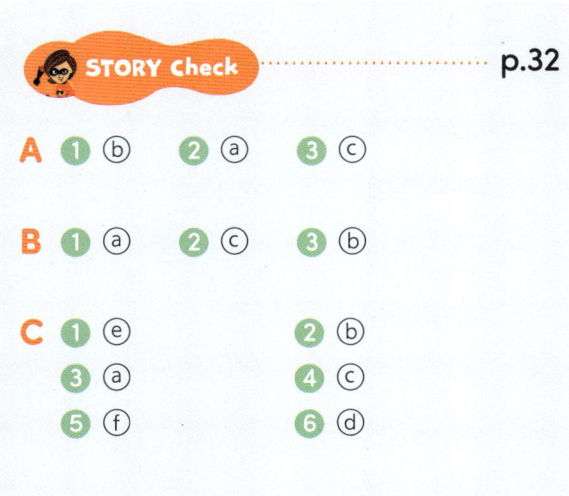

STORY MAP — p.36

① rescued
② spell
③ eyes
④ capture
⑤ lost
⑥ forced
⑦ freed
⑧ stopped

ZOOTOPIA Activities

WORD Check — p.38

A
1. 수달
2. 단서
3. 성취하다
4. 야생의
5. 교활한
6. 체포하다
7. 증명하다
8. 사건

B

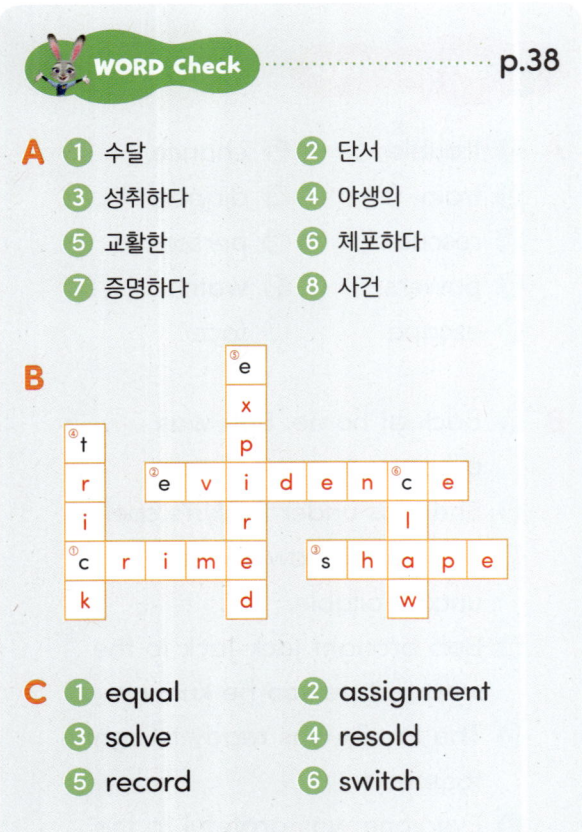

Crossword:
- ⓢ e x p r d (down): expred... — across/down entries: evidence, crime, shape, trick

C
1. equal
2. assignment
3. solve
4. resold
5. record
6. switch

SENTENCE Check — p.42

A
1. paws
2. assignment
3. pay
4. crime
5. plan
6. wrong
7. town
8. turn
9. become
10. partners

B
1. Anyone can be anything!
2. Judy wanted to do a good job.
3. That night, Judy went to bed disappointed.
4. Judy had only two days to solve the crime.
5. They were becoming friends.
6. But Nick didn't turn wild.

STORY Check — p.40

A
1. ⓒ, ⓔ
2. ⓐ, ⓓ
3. ⓑ, ⓕ

B
1. created
2. scared
3. lock

C
1. ⓒ
2. ⓓ
3. ⓑ
4. ⓔ
5. ⓐ
6. ⓕ

STORY MAP — p.44

1. missing
2. wild
3. building
4. serum
5. shot
6. arrested

FROZEN 2 Activities

WORD Check — p.46

A
1. 신비한
2. 비슷한
3. 퍼지다
4. 항의하다
5. 조각품
6. 강력한
7. 자장가
8. 단호한

B

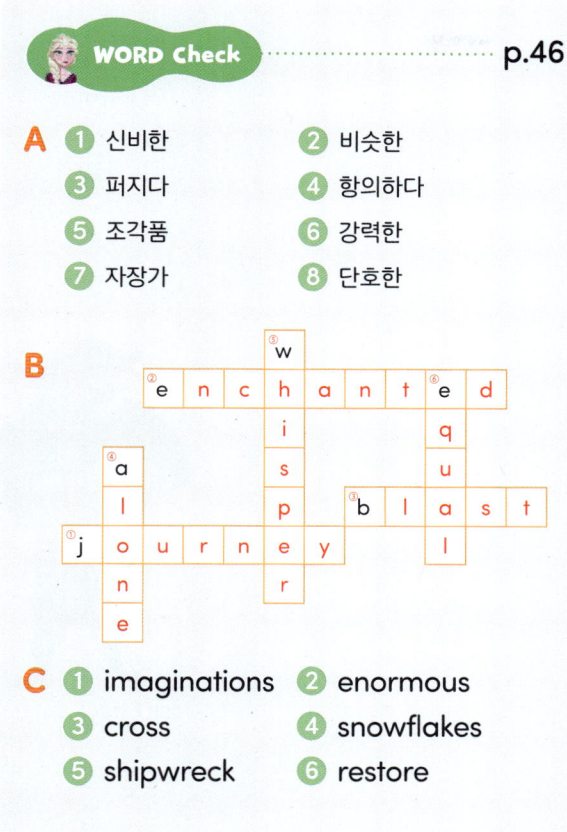

C
1. imaginations
2. enormous
3. cross
4. snowflakes
5. shipwreck
6. restore

SENTENCE Check — p.50

A
1. magical
2. angry
3. working
4. feeding
5. voice
6. shipwreck
7. feared
8. stop
9. questions
10. peace

B
1. The lullaby was about a secret river.
2. Kristoff helped them escape the flames.
3. Anna and Elsa discovered their parents' shipwreck!
4. Elsa couldn't stay any longer.
5. A mutual respect formed between them.
6. It was a signal from Elsa.

STORY Check — p.48

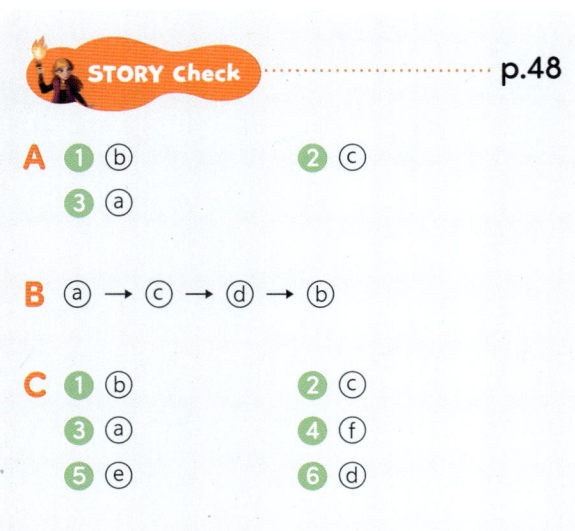

STORY MAP — p.52

① follow
② shipwreck
③ equal
④ signal
⑤ voice
⑥ peace

Activity Book

Part 1 북 퀴즈(Book Quiz)

읽은 내용을 얼마나 잘 이해했는지 북 퀴즈를 풀며 나의 리딩 실력을 점검합니다.
틀린 문제는 스토리북의 해당 내용을 다시 찾아 읽어보세요.

Part 2 학습 액티비티(Activities)

다양한 문제를 풀며 읽은 내용을 되돌아보고 어휘, 스토리 구조, 주요 문장 등을 다집니다.
문제 구성: Word Check • Story Check • Sentence Check • Story Map

  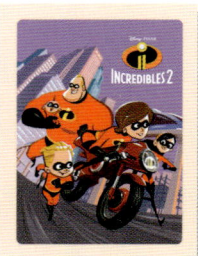  

Copyright©2022 Disney Enterprises, Inc. and Pixar. All rights reserved.

Disney · PIXAR
Story Collection 3

Practice Book

Disney · Pixar Story Collection 3

Word Practice

MOANA

중요 단어를 연습하고, 내가 찾은 단어도 기록해 보세요.

p.12-13

| ocean | 명 대양, 바다 |

✏️

p.14-15

trickster	명 사기꾼
stole	steal(훔치다)의 과거형
island	명 섬
upset	동 속상하게 만들다 (upset-upset-upset)
balance	명 균형 형 균형이 잡힌
dangerous	형 위험한
islander	명 섬사람
beyond	전 ~너머
connection	명 연관성, 연결
creature	명 생물

✏️

p.16-17

notice	동 알아차리다
pick up	줍다, 주워올리다
drop	동 떨어트리다

luckily	튀 다행스럽게도
✎	

p.18-19

heart	명 심장
lead	동 (앞장서서) 안내하다
hidden	형 숨겨진
ancient	형 고대의
spirit	명 영혼, 정령
ancestor	명 조상
voyager	명 항해자, 여행자
✎	

p.20-21

wish	명 소망 동 원하다
across	전 건너서, 가로질러
restore	동 복구하다
sail	명 항해 동 항해하다
especially	튀 특히
storm	명 폭풍

Moana 3

p.22-23

faraway	형 멀리 떨어진
expect	동 예상하다, 기대하다

p.24-25

make sure	확실하게 하다
promise	동 약속하다
return	동 돌아오다
bandit	명 노상강도

p.26-27

dive	동 다이빙하다
realm	명 영역, 왕국
retrieve	동 되찾다
missing	형 없어진, 분실된
taught	teach(가르치다)의 과거형, 과거분사
current	명 해류
navigate	동 길을 찾다, 항해하다
difficult	형 어려운

p.28–29

reach	동	도달하다, ~에 이르다
instead	부	대신에
lava	명	용암
defeat	동	~를 물리치다

p.30–31

summon	동	소환하다, 불러내다
courage	명	용기

p.32–34

bloom	동	꽃을 피우다
complete	동	완료하다
transform into	동	바뀌다, 변형하다
hawk	명	매
exactly	부	정확히
leader	명	지도자
wayfinder	명	길을 찾는 사람

Moana 5

중요 단어를 연습하고, 내가 찾은 단어도 기록해 보세요.

p.40-41

단어	품사	뜻
town	명	(소)도시
full	형	가득한
include	동	포함하다
✏️		

p.42-43

단어	품사	뜻
memory	명	기억
relative	명	친척
broken		break(깨다)의 과거분사
husband	명	남편
rule	명	규칙
musician	명	음악가
brave	형	용감한
perform	동	공연하다, 연주하다
✏️		

p.44-45

단어	품사	뜻
tumble	동	굴러 떨어지다
discovery	명	발견
hold	동	잡고 있다

familiar	형 익숙한, 친숙한

p.46-47

destroy	동 파괴하다, 부수다
tomb	명 무덤
famous	형 유명한
hung	hang(매달다)의 과거형
legend	명 전설
strum	명 (현악기를) 퉁기기

p.48-49

skeleton	명 해골
path	명 길
petal	명 꽃잎
living	형 살아 있는
blessing	명 축복
dead	형 죽은
cross	동 건너다, 가로지르다

p.50-51

another	한 또 하나의, 다른
team up	팀을 짜다
polish	명 광택제 동 윤을 내다
look like	~처럼 보이다
travel	동 여행하다 명 여행
look for	~를 찾다

p.52-53

run out of	~을 다 써버리다
turn into	~으로 변하다
ditch	동 버리다
snuck	sneak(살금살금 가다)의 과거형
fiesta	명 축제
tippy-top	아슬아슬한 꼭대기
place	명 장소 동 놓다, 두다
crowd	동 붐비는, 복잡한

p.54–55

belt out	큰 소리로 노래하다
fall into	~에 빠지다, 떨어지다
overjoyed	형 매우 기뻐하는

p.56–57

appear	동 나타나다
argue	동 언쟁하다
poison	동 독살하다 명 독
stolen	steal(훔치다)의 과거분사
shocked	형 충격을 받은
risk	동 ~의 위험을 무릅쓰다 명 위험
truth	명 진실
pit	명 구덩이

p.58–59

written	write(쓰다)의 과거분사
lullaby	명 자장가
daughter	명 딸

unidentified	형 정체불명의	
✏️		

p.60–61

suddenly	부 갑자기	
rescue	명 구출 동 구출하다	
disappear	동 사라지다	
forget	동 잊어버리다	
remind	동 (기억하도록) 상기시키다	
typically	부 보통, 일반적으로	
thrilled	형 아주 신이 난, 흥분한	
✏️		

p.62

alive	형 살아 있는	
at last	마침내	
realize	동 깨닫다	
closer	부 더 가까이	
support	명 지원, 도움	
✏️		

INCREDIBLES 2

중요 단어를 연습하고, 내가 찾은 단어도 기록해 보세요.

p.68-69

단어	품사	뜻
machine	명	기계
rip	동	(거칠게) 찢다
action	명	행동, 조치
grab	동	붙잡다
fight	동	(적과) 싸우다

p.70-71

단어	품사	뜻
trouble	명	곤경, 문제
allow	동	허락하다
undercover	형	잠복한, 위장한
wealthy	형	부유한
propose	동	제안하다
legal	형	합법적인
nervous	형	불안한

p.72-73

단어	품사	뜻
whole	형	모든, 전체의
move	동	움직이다, 움직이게 하다

Incredibles 2 11

floor	명 바닥
waterfall	명 폭포

p.74-75

runaway	형 달아난, 제멋대로 가는
chase	동 뒤쫓다
rooftop	명 옥상
crane	명 기중기
tunnel	명 터널
stretch	동 뻗다, 늘이다
parachute	명 낙하산

p.76-77

exhausted	형 기진맥진한, 지쳐버린
nap	동 낮잠을 자다
noise	명 소음
intruder	명 불청객
criminal	명 범인, 범죄자

commotion	명 소란, 소동	
✏️		
p.78-79 buzz with	~으로 떠들썩하다	
rescue	명 구출 동 구출하다	
attack	동 공격하다	
take over	빼앗다, 탈취하다	
ambassador	명 대사	
✏️		
p.80-81 catch	동 잡다	
trace	동 추적하다	
capture	동 포획하다	
caught	catch(잡다)의 과거형, 과거분사	
destroy	동 파괴하다	
make sure	확실하게 하다	
spell	명 마법, 주문	
✏️		

p.82-83

serious	형 진지한
uncontrollable	형 통제할 수 없는
manage	동 다루다, 감당하다
calm	형 평온한, 잔잔한
hypnotize	동 최면을 걸다
pounce	동 갑자기 덤벼들다

p.84-85

show up	나타나다
just in time	알맞은 때에
whisk	동 재빨리 가져가다
brought	bring(가져오다)의 과거형, 과거분사
flung	fling(거칠게 내던지다)의 과거형, 과거분사
escape	동 탈출하다

p.86-87

toward	전 ~쪽으로, 향하여
crash	명 충돌 동 충돌하다

free	동 풀어 주다 / 형 자유로운
hypnosis	명 최면
battle	동 싸우다 / 명 전투
normal	형 보통의, 정상적인
fierce	형 사나운, 격렬한
opponent	명 상대, 반대자
no match for	~의 상대가 안되다

p.88-89
| reach | 동 ~에 이르다, 도달하다 |
| shore | 명 해변 |

p.90
grateful	형 고마워하는
law	명 법
face	동 직면하다, 맞서다
challenge	명 도전

Incredibles 2

ZOOTOPIA

중요 단어를 연습하고, 내가 찾은 단어도 기록해 보세요.

p.96-97

city	명 도시
shape	명 모양
equal	형 동등한
whether	접 ~인지 아닌지
claw	명 발톱
paw	명 (동물의 발톱이 발린) 발

p.98-99

farm	명 농장
achieve	동 달성하다, 성취하다
join	동 참가하다, 가담하다
assignment	명 임무
hand	동 건네다, 넘겨주다
machine	명 기계
solve	동 (문제·곤경을) 해결하다

p.100-101

| sharp | 형 날카로운 |

expired	형 만료된	
hundreds of	수백의	
treat	명 간식	
desperate	형 간절히 필요로 하는	
cash	명 현금, 돈	
pay	동 지불하다	

p.102–103
trick	동 속이다 명 속임수	
melt	동 녹다, 녹이다	
create	동 만들다	
resell	동 되팔다	
profit	명 이익	

p.104–105
disappointed	형 실망한	
plan	동 계획하다 명 계획	
crime	명 범죄	

chance	명 기회
missing	형 실종된, 사라진
agree	동 동의하다
grateful	형 고마워하는

p.106-107

recently	부 최근에
convince	동 설득하다, 납득시키다
record	동 녹음하다
shady	형 수상한
deal	명 거래
gather	동 모으다
clue	명 단서, 실마리
otter	명 수달

p.108-109

wrong	형 틀린, 잘못된
wild	형 야생의, 사나운

escape	동 탈출하다	
case	명 (경찰이 조사 중인) 사건	
prove	동 증명하다	

p.110-111

next	형 다음의	
security	명 보안	
edge	명 가장자리, 모서리	
include	동 포함하다	
savage	형 야만적인, 몹시 사나운	

p.112-113

abandoned	형 버려진	
distract	동 주의를 돌리다	
guard	명 경비원	
laboratory	명 실험실	
serum	명 세럼	
cause	동 ~을 야기하다	

mammal	명 포유동물

p.114–115

grab	통 붙잡다, 움켜잡다
predator	명 포식자
citizen	명 시민
lock up	~를 철창 안에 가두다
shoot	통 (총 등을) 쏘다
fill	통 (가득) 채우다
expect	통 예상하다, 기대하다

p.116–118

switch with	~와 바꾸다
evidence	명 증거
arrest	통 체포하다
cure	통 치유하다
dumb	형 바보 같은
sly	형 교활한, 음흉한

FROZEN 2

중요 단어를 연습하고, 내가 찾은 단어도 기록해 보세요.

p.124-125

kingdom	명 왕국
lullaby	명 자장가
sing	동 노래하다
children	명 (child의 복수형) 아이들

p.126-127

answer	명 해답 동 대답하다
past	명 과거 형 지난
imagination	명 상상력
discover	동 발견하다
magical	형 마법의
mysterious	형 신비한
voice	명 목소리
call	동 부르다

p.128-129

| realize | 동 깨닫다 |
| north | 부 북쪽으로 명 북쪽 |

enormous	형 거대한
blast	명 폭발
clear	형 분명한, 확실한
mean	동 의미하다

p.130-131

cliff	명 절벽
awaken	동 깨다, 깨우다
spirit	명 영혼
warn	동 경고하다
enchanted	형 마법에 걸린
forest	명 숲
nomadic	형 유목의

p.132-133

follow	동 따라가다
whoosh	동 '쉭' 소리를 내며 지나가다
reveal	동 드러내다

similar	형 비슷한	
different	형 다른	
while	접 ~하는 동안	p.134–135
mighty	형 강력한, 힘센	
appear	동 나타나다	
spread	동 확산되다, 번지다	
escape	동 탈출하다	p.136–137
flame	명 불길, 불꽃	
calm	동 진정시키다	
snowflake	명 눈송이	
hear	동 듣다	
continue	동 계속하다	
journey	명 여행	
stay	동 그대로 있다, 머무르다	

p.138-139

- **shipwreck** 명 난파선
- **understand** 동 이해하다
- **lose** 동 잃다
- **rest** 명 나머지
- **alone** 형 부 혼자, 외로운

p.140-141

- **form** 동 만들어 내다, 형성하다
- **carry** 동 나르다
- **protest** 동 항의하다
- **accidentally** 부 우연히
- **steer** 동 조종하다
- **quiet** 형 조용한
- **pass** 동 지나가다, 통과하다

p.142-143

- **determine** 형 단호한, 확고한
- **reach** 동 ~에 이르다

cross	동 건너다, 가로지르다
✏️	

p.144-145

rear up	자리를 박차고 일어서다
fierce	형 격렬한
battle	명 전투
equal	형 동등한
respect	명 존경 동 존경하다
sculpture	명 조각상
signal	명 신호
question	명 질문
✏️	

p.146

whisper	명 속삭임 동 속삭이다
inner	형 내부의, 안쪽의
restore	동 회복시키다
harmony	명 조화
✏️	

Disney · Pixar Story Collection 3

Sentence Practice

MOANA

빈칸에 알맞은 단어를 채워 문장을 완성하세요.

1. 모투누이의 모아나는 어렸을 때부터 바다를 사랑했어요.
   Even when she was little, Moana of Motunui LOVED the _____.

2. 그녀는 탈라 할머니의 이야기를 듣는 것도 아주 좋아했어요.
   She also loved _____ing to Gramma Tala's stories.

3. 모아나가 가장 좋아하는 것은 반신반인 사기꾼인 마우이 이야기였어요. 마우이는 어머니 섬인 테피티의 심장을 훔쳤어요.
   Moana's favorite was about the trickster _____ Maui, who stole the heart of the mother island, Te Fiti.

4. 할머니 말씀에 따르면 마우이가 그 심장을 훔쳐서 자연의 균형을 뒤엎어 놓았다고 했어요.
   According to Gramma, Maui upset the _____ of nature by stealing the heart.

5. 모아나의 아빠인 투이 족장은 바다가 위험하다고 생각했어요.
   Moana's dad, _____ Tui, believed the ocean was dangerous.

6. 섬에 사는 사람들은 암초 너머까지 항해하는 것이 금지되어 있었어요!
   The islanders were forbidden to sail beyond the _____!

7. 하지만 어린 모아나는 자신이 바다와 그 속의 모든 생물들과 깊이 연결되어 있다는 느낌을 받았어요.
   But little Moana felt a deep _____ to the ocean, and to all the creatures who belonged in it.

8. 모아나는 언제나 돕고 싶었어요. 그리고 바다는 그것을 알아챘어요! 바다는 모아나에게 특별한 선물을 주었어요.
   She always wanted to help. And the ocean noticed! It gave Moana a special _____.

9. 투이 족장이 모아나를 들어올려 안았을 때, 모아나는 그 선물을 떨어뜨렸어요. 다행히 누군가가 그것을 집어 들었어요.
   When Chief Tui _____ed up Moana, she dropped the gift. Luckily, someone else picked it up.

Word Box

listen	balance	demigod	ocean	chief
동 듣다	명 균형	명 반신반인	명 바다	명 족장
gift	connection	reef	pick up	
명 선물	명 연결	명 암초	~을 들어올리다	

10 그것은 탈라 할머니였어요! 그녀는 바다의 그 선물이 테 피티의 심장이라고 믿었어요!

It was Gramma Tala! She believed the ocean's gift was the _____ of Te Fiti!

11 모아나는 그녀의 부족민들을 이끌고 아버지의 규칙을 따르기 위해 노력하면서 성장했어요.

As she grew, Moana worked hard to help _____ her people and follow her father's rules.

12 모아나가 열 여섯 살이 되자, 탈라 할머니는 그녀를 따로 한쪽으로 데려갔어요.

But when Moana turned sixteen, Gramma Tala took her _____.

13 "이제 네가 어떤 운명을 타고 났는지 알아야 할 때다." 할머니가 말했어요.

"It's time to _____ who you were meant to be," Gramma said.

14 할머니는 모아나를 비밀 동굴로 데려갔는데, 그곳은 오래된 카누들로 가득 차 있었어요.

She led Moana to a hidden _____ ... full of ancient canoes.

15 모아나가 북을 두드리자 그녀는 조상의 혼을 느낄 수 있었어요.

When Moana started drumming, she could feel the spirits of her _____s.

16 그들은 길을 찾는 사람들이었어요. 바다 위의 항해자였죠!

They were wayfinders— _____s on the ocean!

17 탈라 할머니의 마지막 소원은 모아나가 바다를 떠나 마우이를 찾고, 테 피티의 심장을 되찾는 것이었어요.

Gramma Tala's last wish was for Moana to journey across the ocean, find Maui, and _____ the heart of Te Fiti.

18 그래서 모아나는 그 심장을 목걸이 안에 안전하게 담고, 항해를 떠났어요.

So, with the heart safe inside her necklace, Moana set _____.

Word Box

heart	sail	aside	restore	cavern
명 심장	명 항해 통 항해하다	부 한쪽으로	통 복구하다, 되찾게 하다	명 큰 동굴
ancestor	voyager	learn	lead	
명 조상	명 항해자, 여행자	통 ~을 알게 되다	통 이끌다	

19 하지만 넓은 바다를 항해하는 것은 쉽지 않은 일이었어요. 특히 폭풍이 몰아칠 때는요!

But sailing on the open ocean was not easy for Moana—especially when a _____ hit!

20 모아나와 그녀의 배는 먼 섬으로 쓸려갔는데, 그녀는 그곳에서 반신반인 마우이를 만났어요!

Moana and her boat _____ed up on a faraway island, where she met Maui the demigod!

21 그는 모아나가 예상했던 대로 행동하지 않았어요. 마우이는 모아나의 배를 훔쳤어요!

He was NOT what Moana _____ed. Maui stole Moana's boat!

22 그러나 그가 항해를 떠나려 하자, 바다는 모아나도 그와 함께 가도록 했어요. 바다는 그들이 함께 하기를 원했어요.

But when he _____ to sail away, the ocean made sure Moana went with him. The ocean wanted them to work together.

23 마우이는 테피티의 심장을 돌려놓는 것을 돕겠다고 약속했어요. 모아나가 마우이의 마법 갈고리를 찾는 것을 돕겠다는 조건으로요.

Maui promised to help return the heart of Te Fiti only if Moana helped him find his magic _____.

24 하지만 우선 코코넛 껍질을 가진 사나운 강도 무리인 카카모라에게서 빠져나와야 했어요.

But first, they had to get past the Kakamora, an army of wild, coconut-clad _____s.

25 그 다음에는 괴물들의 영역인 랄로타이로 뛰어들어야 했어요!

Then they had to dive into Lalotai... the _____ of monsters!

26 모아나는 재빨리 생각을 해내서 게 괴물인 타마토아를 속였고, 모아나와 마우이는 잃어버린 갈고리를 되찾았어요.

Thinking fast, Moana tricked Tamatoa, a crab monster, and she and Maui _____d the missing fishhook.

Word Box

| **fishhook** 명 낚시 바늘, 갈고리 | **wash up** ~로 쓸려 오다 | **storm** 명 폭풍 | **tried** try(~하려 하다)의 과거형 |
| **realm** 명 영역 | **bandit** 명 강도, 무법자 | **retrieve** 동 되찾다 | **expect** 동 예상하다 |

27. 항해하는 동안 마우이는 모아나에게 길을 찾는 방법을 알려줬어요. 그것은 해와 별, 달과 해류를 이용해 항해하는 방법이었어요.

Along the way, Maui taught Moana how to wayfind, which is to use the sun, the stars, the moon, and the ocean current to _____.

28. 여정이 너무나 어려워졌을 때, 탈라 할머니의 영혼이 돌아왔어요.

And when the journey became too difficult, the spirit of Gramma Tala _____ed.

29. "네가 어떤 사람이 되기 위해 태어났는지 알아야 한단다." 할머니의 영혼이 모아나에게 말했어요.

"Know who you are meant to be," Gramma's _____ told Moana.

30. 모아나와 마우이가 마침내 테 피티에 도착했을 때, 그 어머니 섬은 사라지고 없었어요.

When Moana and Maui finally _____ed Te Fiti, the mother island was gone.

31. 대신 테 카라는 이름의 용암 괴물이 있었어요!

Instead, there was a _____ monster named Te Kā!

32. 마우이와 모아나는 모든 것을 시도했지만 테 카를 물리칠 수 없었어요.

Maui and Moana tried everything, but they could not _____ Te Kā.

33. 그때 모아나에게 생각이 하나 떠올랐어요. 모든 용기를 내, 모아나는 그 심장을 테 카에게 주었어요.

Then Moana had an idea. Summoning all her _____, Moana gave the heart to Te Kā.

34. 그리고 테 카는 자신이 무엇이었는지 기억해 냈어요. 그녀는 테피티였어요!

And Te Kā _____ed who she was meant to be... She was Te Fiti!

35. 심장이 돌아오자 테 피티에는 다시 한번 꽃이 피었어요. 세상은 다시 균형을 이루게 되었어요.

With her heart restored, Te Fiti _____ed once again. The world was back in balance.

Word Box

bloom	remember	spirit	return	lava
동 꽃을 피우다	동 기억하다	명 영혼	동 돌아오다	명 용암
navigate	courage	reach	defeat	
동 항해하다	명 용기	동 도달하다	동 물리치다	

Moana

36 모아나와 마우이는 작별 인사를 했어요. 그들이 함께 한 여정이 완료되었어요.

Moana and Maui said goodbye. Their journey together was ☐.

37 마우이는 매로 변신해서 날아가 버렸어요. 모아나도 자신의 가족과 부족민들에게 돌아갈 시간이 되었어요.

Maui ☐ed into a hawk and flew away. It was time for Moana to return to her people.

38 모투누이에서 온 어린 소녀는 이제 자신이 무엇이 되기 위해 태어난 사람인지 정확히 알게 되었어요.

The young girl from Motunui now knew ☐ who she was meant to be.

39 그녀는 딸이었고, 지도자였고, 길을 찾는 사람이었어요. 그녀는 모아나였어요!

She was a daughter, a ☐, and a wayfinder. She was Moana!

Word Box

exactly	transform	completed	leader
분 정확히	통 바뀌다, 변형하다	형 완료된	명 지도자

COCO

빈칸에 알맞은 단어를 채워 문장을 완성하세요.

1. 산타 세실리아의 작은 도시에 미겔 리베라라는 이름의 소년이 살고 있었어요.
   In the small _____ of Santa Cecilia, there lived a boy named Miguel Rivera.

2. 그의 집은 가족들로 가득했는데, 증조 할머니인 마마 코코도 계셨어요.
   His house was _____ of family, including his great-grandmother, Mamá Coco.

3. 매년 망자의 날에 그의 가족들은 돌아가신 친척들에 대한 추억을 나누었어요.
   Every year on Dia de los Muertos, the Day of the Dead, his family shared the memories of relatives who had _____ed on.

4. 미겔의 할머니는 그의 고조 할머니인 마마 이멜다의 이야기를 해주곤 했는데, 마마 이멜다는 음악가인 남편 때문에 마음 아파했다고 했어요.
   Miguel's abuelita would tell the story of his great-great-grandmother, Mamá Imelda, whose heart had been broken by her _____ husband.

5. 그 때문에, 리베라 집안에는 규칙 하나가 생겼어요. 음악 금지!
   Because of him, there was one _____ in the Rivera household: NO MUSIC!

6. 하지만 미겔은 음악을 사랑했어요. 그는 그의 비밀 은신처에서 그가 가장 좋아하는 음악가인 에르네스토 델라 크루즈의 비디오를 보면서 기타 치는 법을 배웠어요.
   But Miguel LOVED music. In his secret _____, he learned to play guitar by watching videos of his favorite musician, Ernesto de la Cruz.

7. 영감을 받은 느낌에 용기가 생겨서, 미겔과 그의 개 단테는 집을 살금살금 빠져나와 지역 경연 대회에서 연주하기로 했어요.
   Feeling _____ and brave, Miguel and his dog, Dante, snuck out of the house to perform in a local talent show.

8. 하지만 나가는 길에 단테가 가족의 제단으로 뛰어 올랐어요.
   But on the way out, Dante jumped onto the family ofrenda, or _____.

Word Box

| town 명 도시 | musician 명 음악가 | altar 명 제단 | full 형 가득한, 많은 |
| rule 명 규칙 | inspired 형 영감을 받은 | hideout 명 비밀 은신처 | pass on 돌아가시다 |

Coco 33

⑨ 마마 이멜다의 사진이 요란한 소리와 함께 굴러 떨어졌어요!

Mamá Imelda's photo [tumble]d down with a crash!

⑩ 그때 미겔은 한 가지 발견을 했어요.

That was when Miguel made a [discovery].

⑪ 마마 이멜다의 남편은 기타를 들고 있었어요. 그리고 굉장히 낯익어 보였어요!

Mama Imelda's husband was holding a guitar—and it looked very [familiar]!

⑫ "마마 코코의 아빠가 에르네스토 델라 크루즈였어!" 미겔이 외쳤어요. "나는 음악가가 될 거야!"

"Mamá Coco's papá was Ernesto de la Cruz!" Miguel [cried]. "I'm going to be a musician!"

⑬ 하지만 가족 규칙 때문에 할머니는 그의 기타를 가져가서 부숴버렸어요.

But because of their family rule, his abuelita took his guitar and [destroy]ed it.

⑭ 미겔은 최대한 빨리 달려서 에르네스토의 무덤으로 갔어요. 그곳에는 유명한 기타가 아직 걸려 있었어요.

Miguel ran as fast as he could to Ernesto's [tomb], where the famous guitar still hung.

⑮ 그것을 벽에서 떼어내며 미겔이 말했어요. "화내지 말아 주세요. 당신처럼 음악가가 되려면 이것이 필요해요!"

Taking it off the wall, he said, "Please don't be [mad]. I need this to be a musician like you!"

⑯ 그리고 그는 그 전설의 기타를 한 번 퉁겨 연주했어요. 갑자기 미겔은 해골들을 알아차렸어요!

And he gave the legend's guitar a [strum]. All of a sudden, Miguel noticed all the skeletons!

⑰ 해골들은 망자의 날을 맞아 살아 있는 친척들을 방문하기 위해 금잔화 꽃잎 길을 따라온 참이었어요.

They had followed the path of marigold [petal]s to visit their living relatives for Día de los Muertos.

Word Box

mad	cried	discovery	destroy	familiar
형 몹시 화가 난	cry(외치다)의 과거형	명 발견	동 부수다	형 낯익은
tumble	tomb	petal	strum	
동 굴러 떨어지다	명 무덤	명 꽃잎	명 (현악기를) 퉁겨서 연주하기	

18 살아 있는 자들의 땅으로 가려면 돌아가신 가족 중 한 사람의 축복을 받아야 했어요.

To return to the Land of the Living, Miguel would need a _____ from one of his dead family members.

19 그래서 미겔과 단테는 금잔화 다리를 건너 죽은 자들의 땅으로 향했어요.

So he and Dante _____ed the Marigold Bridge into the Land of the Dead.

20 미겔은 마마 이멜다를 찾았지만, 그녀는 만약 미겔이 음악가가 되고 싶은 거라면 축복하지 않겠다고 말했어요.

Miguel _____ Mamá Imelda, but she said she wouldn't give him her blessing if he wanted to be a musician.

21 미겔은 다른 방법을 찾아야 했어요.

Miguel had to find another _____.

22 그래서 그는 에르네스토 델라 크루즈를 알고 있는 헥토르라는 해골과 팀을 짜기로 했어요.

So he _____ed up with a skeleton named Héctor, who said he knew Ernesto de la Cruz.

23 헥토르는 구두약으로 미겔을 해골처럼 보이게 만들었어요.

With some _____ _____, Héctor made Miguel look like a skeleton.

24 그들은 에르네스토를 찾아 이곳저곳을 돌아다녔어요.

They traveled all over _____ing for Ernesto.

25 심지어 그들은 경연 대회에서 공연도 했어요! 하지만 미겔의 시간은 점점 끝나가고 있었어요.

They even performed together in a talent show! But Miguel was running out of _____.

26 만약 에르네스토의 축복을 받지 못한다면 미겔은 진짜 해골로 변해서 다시는 집에 돌아가지 못할 거예요!

If he didn't get Ernesto's blessing soon, he'd _____ into a real skeleton and never get home!

Word Box

found	cross	blessing	way	turn into
find(찾다)의 과거형	통 건너다	명 축복	명 방법	~으로 변하다
shoe polish	time	look for	team up	
명 구두약	명 시간	~을 찾다	팀을 짜다	

Coco 35

27 그래서 미겔은 자신의 힘으로 고조 할아버지를 찾기 위해 헥토르를 떠났어요.

So he _____ed Héctor to find his great-great-grandpa on his own.

28 미겔은 높은 건물의 아슬아슬한 꼭대기에서 열리는 에르네스토의 축제로 살금살금 들어갔어요.

Miguel snuck into Ernesto's _____ at the tippy-top of a tall tower.

29 하지만 사람들로 너무 붐벼서 미겔은 에르네스토에게 다가갈 수가 없었어요. 그래서 미겔은 힘차게 노래를 불렀어요!

But the place was so _____, Miguel couldn't get to Ernesto. So Miguel belted out a song!

30 모두가 지켜봤어요. 미겔이 노래하다가 에르네스토의 풀장에 빠지는 모습을요. 해골들은 그가 살아 있는 소년인 것을 알아차렸어요.

Everyone watched as he sang… and fell into Ernesto's _____. The skeletons saw that he was a living boy.

31 에르네스토는 매우 기뻐했어요! "내게 고조 손자가 있다니!"

Ernesto was _____! "I have a great-great-grandson!"

32 하지만 그때 헥토르가 나타났어요. 그리고 그 두 남자가 다투는 동안 미겔은 어두운 진실을 알게 되었어요.

But then Héctor appeared, and as the two men _____d, Miguel learned the dark truth.

33 그의 고조 할아버지는 헥토르를 독살하고 그의 노래들을 훔쳐서 유명해진 것이었어요.

His great-great-grandpa had _____ed Héctor and stolen his songs to become famous.

34 미겔은 에르네스토의 얼굴이 차갑게 변하는 것을 보고 충격을 받았어요.

Miguel was _____ to see Ernesto's face turn cold.

35 에르네스토는 세상이 진실을 알게 되는 위험을 무릅쓸 수 없었다고 설명했어요.

Ernesto explained that he couldn't _____ letting the world know the truth.

Word Box

fiesta	ditch	pool	risk	overjoyed
명 (스페인어권 국가의) 축제	동 버리다, 관계를 끊다	명 풀장, 수영장	동 ~의 위험을 무릅쓰다	형 매우 기뻐하는
poison	argue	shocked	crowded	
동 독살하다	동 언쟁을 하다, 다투다	형 충격을 받은	형 붐비는, 복잡한	

㊱ 그러더니 그는 미겔과 헥토르를 깜깜한 구덩이 속으로 던져 버렸어요.
Then he [threw] Miguel and Héctor down, down, down—into a dark pit.

㊲ 헥토르는 자신이 작곡한 노래들은 모두 그의 가족을 위한 것이었다고 말했어요.
Héctor told Miguel that the songs he'd [written] were all for his family.

㊳ 그리고 그 중에는 그의 딸 코코에게 불러주던 특별한 자장가도 있었어요. 곡명은 '날 기억해 줘.'였어요.
And there was a special [lullaby] he would always sing for his daughter, Coco. "Remember me."

㊴ 미겔은 마마 이멜다의 사진과 그 정체를 알 수 없는 남자를 떠올렸어요.
Miguel thought of Mamá Imelda's photo and the [unidentified] man.

㊵ "당신이군요! 헥터, 당신이 내 고조 할아버지예요!"
"It's you! Héctor, YOU are my [great-great-grandpa]!"

㊶ 갑자기 마마 이멜다와 단테가 그들을 구출하러 왔어요.
Suddenly, Mamá Imelda and Dante came to their [rescue].

㊷ 그러나 헥토르는 사라지기 시작했어요. 그의 딸이 그를 잊기 시작했던 거예요.
But Héctor began to [disappear]. His daughter was starting to forget him.

㊸ 마마 이멜다와 헥토르는 미겔을 축복해 그를 집으로 돌려 보냈어요.
Mamá Imelda and Héctor [sent] Miguel home with their blessing.

㊹ 살아 있는 자들의 땅으로 돌아온 미겔은 마마 코코에게 달려갔어요. 그는 할머니를 위해 노래 '날 기억해줘'를 불렀어요. 그녀의 아빠를 생각나게 해주려고요.
Back in the Land of the Living, Miguel rushed to Mamá Coco. He sang "Remember Me" to [remind] her of her papá.

Word Box

sent send(보내다)의 과거형	**lullaby** 명 자장가	**threw** throw(던지다)의 과거형	**unidentified** 형 정체불명의	**great-great-grandpa** 명 고조 할아버지
written write(작곡하다)의 과거분사	**disappear** 동 사라지다	**remind** 동 생각나게 하다	**rescue** 명 구출	

45 할머니는 평소에 말을 하지 않았기 때문에 미겔은 할머니가 노래를 따라 부르기 시작하자 아주 신이 났어요.

She typically didn't talk much so Miguel was [   ] when she began to sing along!

46 마마 코코는 아빠에 대한 이야기를 친척들과 나누면서 아빠에 대한 추억이 계속 살아 있도록 했어요.

Mamá Coco kept her papá's memory [   ] by sharing stories of him with her relatives.

47 마침내 리베라 가족들은 음악이 그들을 서로 더 가까이 해줄 수 있다는 사실을 깨달았어요.

At last, the Riveras realized that music could bring them [   ] together.

48 그리고 이제 미겔은 그의 꿈을 쫓아 음악가가 될 수 있다는 것을 알았어요. 가족들의 지지를 받으면서요.

And now Miguel knew he could follow his dream and become a musician—with his family's [   ].

Word Box

closer	alive	thrilled	support
뷔 더 가까이	헝 살아 있는	헝 아주 신이 난	몡 지지, 도움

INCREDIBLES 2

빈칸에 알맞은 단어를 채워 문장을 완성하세요.

1. 인크레더블은 슈퍼 히어로 가족이었어요.
   The incredibles were a _____ of supers.

2. 기계 한 대가 도시에 거칠게 돌진하자, 그들은 휙 움직여 행동을 개시했어요!
   When a machine started ripping up the city, they sprang into _____!

3. 인크레더블 씨와 엘라스티걸이 그것을 멈추려 하는 동안, 그들의 아이들 바이올렛과 대쉬는 아기 잭잭을 단단히 붙잡았어요.
   While Mr. Incredible and Elastigirl tried to stop it, their kids Violet and Dash _____bed baby Jack-Jack.

4. 그들의 친구인 프로존도 싸움에 참여했어요! 인크레더블 가족은 그 기계를 멈추게 했지만 큰 문제에 처했어요.
   Their friend Frozone joined in the fight! The Incredibles stopped the machine but got in big _____.

5. 슈퍼 히어로들은 그들의 힘을 쓰는 것이 허락되지 않았거든요.
   Supers were not _____ed to use their powers.

6. 인크레더블 씨와 엘라스티걸은 밥과 헬렌 파로서 아이들과 함께 비밀 첩보원 생활로 돌아갈 수밖에 없었어요.
   Mr. Incredible and Elastigirl had no choice but to return to their _____ lives as Bob and Helen Parr, along with their kids.

7. 하지만 그때 윈스턴 데버라는 이름의 부유한 사업가와 그의 여동생인 에블린이 슈퍼 히어로들을 다시 합법적으로 만들자고 제안했어요.
   But then a wealthy businessman named Winston Deavor and his sister, Evelyn, proposed a plan to make Supers _____ again.

8. 엘라스티걸이 그 첫 번째 임무를 맡게 되었어요.
   Elastigirl would get the first _____.

Word Box

family	assignment	grab	action	allow
명 가족	명 임무	동 붙잡다	명 행동, 조치	동 ~을 허락하다
legal	undercover	trouble		
형 합법적인	형 잠복한, 위장의	명 곤경, 문제		

9 그녀는 긴장됐어요. 하지만 이것은 그녀의 가족과 모든 슈퍼 히어로들을 도울 기회였어요.

She was _____, but this was her chance to help her Family—and all Supers.

10 윈스턴은 엘라스티걸과 일하게 되어 아주 신이 났어요. 그래서 그의 저택 중 한 곳에 그녀의 가족이 머물러도 좋다고 했어요.

Winston was so excited to work with Elastigirl, he allowed her whole family to stay in one of his _____s.

11 대쉬는 그곳을 매우 좋아했어요! 그는 리모콘을 사용해 바닥을 움직이고 폭포를 작동시켰어요.

Dash loved it! He used a remote control to move the _____s and turn on the waterfalls.

12 엘라스티걸은 출근 첫날, 제멋대로 달려가는 기차를 발견했어요!

On Elastigirl's first day at her new job, she _____ted a runaway train!

13 그녀는 엘라스티 사이클에 올라타서 도시를 가로질러 기차를 쫓아갔어요.

She _____ped onto her Elasticycle and chased the train through the city.

14 그녀는 옥상 위를 재빨리 움직여서 크레인 위를 질주했고… 그리고는 터널을 통과하여 나아갔어요.

She _____d over rooftops... zoomed up a crane... and zipped through a tunnel...

15 그리고 마침내 낙하산을 펼쳐 기차의 속도를 줄였어요. 기차가 선로를 이탈하기 바로 직전에요!

...until finally, she stretched into a _____ and slowed down the train—right before it ran off the tracks!

16 한편 밥은 집에서 기진맥진한 상태가 되어 있었어요.

Back at home, Bob was _____.

17 숙제를 도와주고, 기저귀를 갈고, 드라마 같은 10대 청소년의 일상을 다루는 것은 그를 녹초가 되게 만들었어요.

Helping with homework, changing diapers, and dealing with teenage drama really _____ed him out.

Word Box

mansion 명 대저택	**scramble** 동 재빨리 움직이다	**nervous** 형 긴장한	**hop** 동 (탈 것에) 타다	**spot** 동 발견하다
floor 명 바닥	**parachute** 명 낙하산	**knock out** ~를 녹초가 되게 만들다	**exhausted** 형 기진맥진한, 지쳐버린	

⑱ 밥이 잠깐 자는 동안 잭잭은 TV를 보았어요.

While Bob was [   ]ping, Jack-Jack watched TV.

⑲ 그는 그때 뒷마당에서 어떤 소리를 들었어요. 침입자였어요!

Then he heard a noise in the backyard. It was an [   ]!

⑳ 잭잭은 그 범인을 막으려고 했어요.

Jack-Jack tried to stop the [   ].

㉑ 밥은 소란을 듣고 밖으로 달려 나왔어요.

Bob heard the commotion and ran [   ].

㉒ 그는 자신의 눈을 믿을 수가 없었어요. "너… 능력이… 있구나!"

He couldn't believe his eyes. "You... have... [   ]s!"

㉓ 다음 날, 도시는 엘라스티걸의 놀라운 구조 소식으로 떠들썩했어요.

The next day, the city [   ]ed with the news of Elastigirl's amazing rescue.

㉔ 그녀가 첫 TV 인터뷰를 하는 동안에, 스크린슬레이버라고 불리는 강력한 악당이 공격을 했어요.

During her first TV interview, a super [   ] called the Screenslaver attacked.

㉕ 그는 대사의 헬기를 빼앗았어요. 엘라스티걸은 쏜살같이 달려나가 대사를 구해냈어요!

He took over an [   ]'s helicopter. Elastigirl raced off and rescued the ambassador!

㉖ 엘라스티걸은 스크린슬레이버를 잡아야 했어요. 에블린의 도움으로, 그녀는 은신처로 향하는 악당의 신호를 쫓아갔어요.

Elastigirl still needed to catch the Screenslaver. With Evelyn's help, she traced the villain's [   ] to his lair.

㉗ 그녀는 건물을 누비며 악당을 쫓아 붙잡았어요. 하지만 무언가 잘못된 느낌이었어요.

She chased him through the building and [   ]d him! But something didn't feel right.

Word Box

intruder	power	nap	criminal	outside
명 불법 침입자	명 (신체적·정신적) 능력	통 잠깐 자다	명 범인	부 밖으로, 밖에
villain	capture	ambassador	signal	buzz with
명 악당	통 붙잡다, 포획하다	명 대사	명 신호	~으로 떠들썩하다

28 엘라스티걸은 자신이 엉뚱한 사람을 잡았다는 것을 깨달았어요. 에블린 데버가 진짜 스크린슬레이버였던 거예요!

Elastigirl realized she'd caught the [_____] person—Evelyn Deavor was the real Screenslaver!

29 에블린은 오빠의 계획을 망쳐서 슈퍼 히어로들이 합법적인 존재가 되지 못하게 하고 싶었어요.

Evelyn wanted to [_____] her brother's plan and make sure Supers were never legal again.

30 눈 깜짝할 사이에 에블린은 엘라스티걸에게 최면 고글을 씌웠어요!

In a [_____], Evelyn put Hypno-Goggles on Elastigirl!

31 엘라스티걸은 에블린이 건 마법에 걸렸어요.

She was under Evelyn's [_____].

32 한편 밥은 잭잭 때문에 많은 도움이 필요했어요. 그 아기의 능력을 통제할 수 없었거든요!

Meanwhile, Bob needed some serious help with Jack-Jack. The baby's powers were [_____]!

33 밥은 그가 아는 사람들 중 가장 똑똑한 사람을 데려왔어요. 에드나 모드였죠.

Bob brought him to the [_____] person he knew: Edna Mode.

34 에드나는 잭잭의 능력을 감당하는 데 도움을 줄 특수한 슈퍼 복장과 추적 장치를 만들었어요.

Edna made a special Supersuit and tracker to help [_____] Jack-Jack's powers.

35 집에서는 마침내 모든 것이 평온해졌어요. 그때 에블린이 전화로 엘라스티걸은 곤경에 처해 있다고 말했어요!

Everything was finally [_____] at home. Then Evelyn called and said Elastigirl was in trouble!

36 밥은 프로존에게 아이들을 부탁하고 급히 달려 나갔어요.

Bob asked Frozone to watch the kids and then [_____]ed away.

Word Box

destroy	spell	in a flash	wrong	uncontrollable
통 망치다	명 마법	눈 깜짝할 사이에	형 엉뚱한, 틀린	형 통제할 수 없는
smartest	calm	manage	rush	
형 가장 똑똑한	형 평온한	통 다루다, 감당하다	통 급하게 가다	

37 인크레더블 씨가 데버의 배에 도착하자, 최면에 걸린 엘라스티걸이 별안간 그에게 덤벼들었어요!

When Mr. Incredible arrived at the Deavors' ship, a hypnotized Elastigirl _____d on him!

38 그녀는 그와 싸웠고 그의 눈에 최면 고글을 씌웠어요.

She _____ him until she could put Hypno-Goggles over his eyes.

39 한편 최면에 걸린 슈퍼 히어로들 한 무리가 아이들을 붙잡기 위해 도착했어요. 프로존이 도움을 주기 위해 제때 나타났어요.

Meanwhile, a group of _____d Supers arrived to capture the kids. Frozone showed up just in time to help.

40 대쉬가 리모컨을 누르자 '쌩!' 하고 놀라운 인크레더블 자동차가 멈춰 섰어요.

Dash clicked a remote, and—zoooom!—the amazing Incredibile _____ed up!

41 그것은 프로존이 슈퍼 히어로들에게 붙잡히는 동안 아이들을 재빨리 태워 데려갔어요.

It _____ed the kids away while Frozone was captured by the Supers.

42 인크레더블 자동차는 아이들을 배로 데려왔어요. 하지만 잭잭은 어디에 있는 것일까요?

The Incredible _____ the kids to the ship. But where was Jack-Jack?

43 대쉬와 바이올렛은 실종된 동생을 추적하고 있었어요! 그리고 그때 최면에 걸린 슈퍼 히어로 한 명이 공격했어요!

Dash and Violet were tracking their _____ brother when a hypnotized Super attacked!

44 바이올렛은 그 슈퍼 히어로에게 날카로운 포스 필드를 힘껏 던져 대쉬와 함께 달아났어요.

Violet _____ razor-sharp force fields at the Super until she and Dash could escape.

45 배에 탄 모든 사람들이 에블린의 사악한 마법에 걸려 있었어요.

Everyone on board was under Evelyn's _____ spell.

Word Box

flung	pull up	hypnotized	whisk	fought
fling(거칠게 던지다)의 과거형	멈추다	형 최면에 걸린	통 재빨리 데려가다	fight(싸우다)의 과거형
pounce	wicked	brought	lost	
통 별안간 덤벼들다	형 사악한	bring(데려오다)의 과거형	형 실종된	

46 그녀는 슈퍼 히어로에게 배의 항로를 도시와 충돌하도록 맞추기를 강요했어요.

She [force]d the Supers to set the ship on a crash course toward the city.

47 갑자기 아이들이 나타났어요. 그들은 부모님을 풀어 주고 프로존을 최면에서 풀려나게 했어요.

Suddenly, the kids appeared. They [free]d their parents and Frozone from the hypnosis.

48 가족들은 함께 싸울 준비가 되었어요! 인크레더블 가족과 프로존은 최면에 걸린 나머지 슈퍼 히어로들과 싸웠어요.

The family was ready to fight together! The Incredibles and Frozone [battle]d the rest of the hypnotized Supers.

49 곧 모두가 정상 상태로 돌아왔어요.

Before long, everyone was back to [normal].

50 그러자 에블린은 도망치려 했어요! 엘라스티걸이 그녀를 쫓아갔어요. 에블린은 사나운 상대였지만, 엘라스티걸의 상대는 되지 못했어요.

Then Evelyn tried to escape! Elastigirl chased after her. Evelyn was a fierce [opponent], but she was no match for Elastigirl.

51 모든 슈퍼 히어로들이 협력해서 배가 도심지에 충돌하는 것을 막았어요.

All the Supers worked together to keep the ship from [crash]ing into the city center.

52 그들은 배를 돌려서 해안에 닿기 직전에 배를 멈췄어요!

They turned the ship around, stopping it just before it reached the [shore]!

53 모두가 슈퍼 히어로들에게 고마워했어요. 시에서는 법을 바꿔 그들이 힘을 다시 쓸 수 있도록 허락했어요.

Everyone was [grateful] to the Supers. The city changed the law, making it legal for them to use their powers again.

54 이제 인크레더블 가족은 어떤 도전에도 맞설 준비가 되었어요. 한 가족으로서 말이에요!

Now the Incredibles were ready to [face] any challenge—as a family!

Word Box

grateful	free	opponent	normal	battle
형 고마워하는	통 풀어 주다	명 상대	형 정상인	통 싸우다
crash	force	shore	face	
통 충돌하다	통 ~를 강요하다	명 해안	통 맞서다	

ZOOTOPIA

빈칸에 알맞은 단어를 채워 문장을 완성하세요.

1 주토피아는 놀라운 도시였어요! 크기와 모양이 각양각색인 온갖 동물들이 함께 행복하게 살고 일했어요.

Zootopia was an _____ city! Animals of all different sizes and shapes lived and worked together happily.

2 발톱이 길든, 발이 작든 모두가 평등했어요.

Everyone was equal, whether they had long _____s or little paws.

3 누구나 무엇이든 될 수 있어요!

Anyone can be _____!

4 버니버로우 농장 출신인 작은 토끼도 꿈꾸던 직업을 성취할 수 있었어요.

Even a small bunny from a farm in Bunnyburrow could _____ her dream job.

5 주디 홉스는 주토피아 경찰청에 합류한 최초의 토끼였어요!

Judy Hopps was the first bunny ever to join the Zootopia Police _____!

6 주디는 그녀의 첫 번째 임무를 기다리며 흥분에 차 깡총깡총 뛰었어요.

Judy hopped with _____ as she waited for her first assignment.

7 하지만 보고 경찰서장이 그녀에게 주차권을 발급하는 기계를 건네 주자 그녀의 귀는 축 늘어졌어요.

But when Police Chief Bogo _____ed her a machine for issuing parking tickets, her ears fell.

8 그녀는 범죄를 해결하고 싶었어요. 주차 위반 단속 요원이 아니라요. 그래도 주디는 일을 잘 하고 싶었어요.

She wanted to _____ crimes, not be a meter maid. Still, Judy wanted to do a good job.

Word Box

claw	anything	amazing	achieve
명 발톱	대 무엇이든	형 놀라운	동 성취하다
hand	department	excitement	solve
동 건네주다	명 청, 부서	명 흥분, 신남	동 해결하다, 풀다

⑨ 그녀는 예리한 청력으로 만료된 미터기를 바로 알아차릴 수 있었고, 그래서 점심 시간 전까지 주차 위반 딱지를 수백 장이나 작성했어요!

Her sharp hearing alerted her to _____ meters, and she wrote hundreds of parking tickets-before lunchtime!

⑩ 정오에 주디는 코끼리만한 크기의 간식을 먹으려고 근처 카페에 갔어요.

At noon, Judy headed to a nearby cafe for an elephant-sized _____.

⑪ 그곳에서 그녀는 특대형 막대 아이스크림을 간절히 원하는 어린 여우를 만났어요.

There she met a little fox who was _____ for a Jumbo-pop.

⑫ 그의 아빠인 닉은 현금이 없어서 주디가 기꺼이 돈을 내주기로 했어요.

His dad, Nick, was out of cash, so Judy _____ed to pay.

⑬ 하지만 곧 주디는 닉이 그녀를 속였다는 것을 알게 됐어요!

But very soon, Judy learned that Nick had _____ed her!

⑭ 그는 특대형 막대 아이스크림을 녹여서 더 작은 아이스크림들을 만들었어요.

He _____ed the Jumbo-pop to create smaller pawpsicles.

⑮ 그리고 그것들을 다시 되팔아 큰 이익을 남겼어요.

Then he _____ those for a big profit.

⑯ 그날 밤, 주디는 실망한 채로 잠자리에 들었어요.

That night, Judy went to bed _____.

⑰ 그날은 그녀의 계획대로 되지 않았어요.

The day hadn't turned out like she'd _____ned.

⑱ 그녀는 범죄와 싸우고 싶었어요. "단 한 번의 기회가 필요해…"

She wanted to fight crime. "I just need one _____…"

Word Box

trick	offer	desperate	treat	plan
통 속이다	통 제공하다	형 간절히 원하는	명 간식	통 계획하다
resold	expired	melt	disappointed	chance
resell(되팔다)의 과거형	형 만료된	통 녹이다	형 실망한	명 기회

19 다음 날 주디는 기회를 잡았어요. 오터튼 부인의 남편이 실종되어서 주디가 그 사건을 맡게 되었어요.

The next day, Judy got her chance. Mrs. Otterton's husband was _____, and Judy offered to take the case.

20 부시장인 벨웨더도 동의했고, 오터튼 부인은 매우 고마워했어요! 하지만 범죄를 해결하는 데 겨우 이틀의 시간이 주어졌어요!

Assistant Mayor Bellwether _____d, and Mrs. Otterton was so grateful! But Judy had only two days to solve the crime!

21 주디는 닉이 최근에 오터튼 씨를 봤다는 사실을 알게 됐어요.

Judy learned that Nick had seen Mr. Otterton _____.

22 그녀는 속임수를 써서 그 여우를 설득하여 자신을 돕도록 했어요.

She _____d the fox to help her by pulling her own trick.

23 그녀는 당근 펜을 이용해 닉이 자신의 수상한 사업 거래에 관해 말하는 것을 녹음했어요! "난 세금을 절대 안 내!"

She used her carrot pen to record him talking about his _____ business deals! "I never pay taxes!"

24 닉은 마지못해 주디를 도와 주토피아 전역에서 단서를 모았고, 그들은 열대우림 지역에 도착했어요.

Reluctantly, Nick helped Judy gather _____s all across Zootopia until they reached the Rainforest District.

25 계획은 그 수달을 마지막으로 본 동물인 만차스 씨를 심문하는 것이었어요.

The plan was to _____ Mr. Manchas, the last animal to have seen the otter.

26 닉과 주디는 만차스 씨를 찾았어요. 하지만 그에게 어떤 문제가 있었어요. 그는 사납게 변해 있었어요!

Nick and Judy found Mr. Manchas, but something was wrong with him. He had gone _____!

Word Box

recently	**agree**	**missing**	**convince**
부 최근에	동 동의하다	형 실종된	동 설득하다
wild	**shady**	**question**	**clue**
형 사나운	형 수상한 구석이 있는	동 심문하다	명 단서

27 닉과 주디는 함께 노력해 달아났어요. 그들은 친구가 되어가고 있었어요!

Nick and Judy worked together and ⬚d. They were becoming friends!

28 그들 모두 이 사건을 해결해서 그들도 중요한 일을 할 수 있다는 것을 증명하고 싶었어요.

Both of them wanted to solve this case and ⬚ they could do important work.

29 주디는 다음 단서를 어떻게 찾아야 할지 알고 있었어요!

Judy knew how to find their next ⬚!

30 방범 카메라에 찍힌 장면을 이용해서, 그녀는 닉을 시 변두리에 있는 무서운 건물로 데려갔어요.

Using security camera ⬚, she led Nick to a scary building on the edge of town.

31 그들은 안에서 실종된 수달을 포함해서 눈빛이 사나운 동물들을 더 찾아냈어요! 이 동물들은 왜 야만스럽게 변했을까요?

Inside, they found more wild-eyed animals—including the missing otter! Why had these animals turned ⬚?

32 한 정보원의 조언에 따라 닉과 주디는 버려진 지하철 역으로 이동했어요.

A tip from an informer led Nick and Judy to an ⬚ subway station.

33 닉이 경비원들의 주의를 딴 데로 돌리는 동안, 주디는 지하철 열차 안으로 슬그머니 들어갔는데 그곳은 비밀 실험실이었어요!

While Nick ⬚ed the guards, Judy slipped into a subway car that was also a secret laboratory!

34 주디는 한 숫양이 꽃을 이용해 세럼을 만드는 것을 보았어요.

Judy saw a ram create a ⬚ using a flower.

35 포유 동물들이 사납게 변하도록 야기한 것은 그 세럼이었어요!

She learned that the serum ⬚d mammals to the wild!

Word Box

escape	footage	lead	prove	cause
통 달아나다	명 장면, 화면	명 실마리, 단서	통 증명하다	통 ~을 야기하다
distract	**abandoned**	**serum**	**savage**	
통 주의를 딴 데로 돌리다	형 버려진, 유기된	명 세럼, 농축액	형 야만적인	

36. 닉과 주디는 그 세럼을 낚아채서 도망치다가 벨웨더 부시장 때문에 궁지에 몰렸어요!
Nick and Judy grabbed the serum and ran until they were [corner]ed by Assistant Mayor Bellwether!

37. 그 교활한 양이 그 세럼을 만들었던 거예요. 발톱과 송곳니를 가진 포식자 동물들이 사나워지면 시민들이 그들을 무서워할 것이라 생각했기 때문이에요.
The sneaky sheep had created the serum because she knew that if animals with claws and fangs—[predator]s—became savage, citizens would be scared of them.

38. 그러면 더 작은 동물들이 포식자 동물들을 잡아 두고 권력을 쥘 수 있으니까요!
Then the smaller animals could [lock] them up and take over!

39. 벨웨더는 세럼으로 가득 찬 작은 화살을 닉에게 쏘았어요!
Bellwether shot a [dart] filled with the serum into Nick!

40. 그 여우는 네 발로 주저앉아 몸을 떨기 시작했어요.
The fox [sank] to all fours and started shaking.

41. 벨웨더는 미소 지었어요. 그녀는 닉이 야만스러워져서 주디를 잡아먹을 것이라 예상했어요!
Bellwether smiled. She [expect]ed Nick to become savage and eat Judy!

42. 그러나 닉은 사납게 변하지 않았어요.
But Nick didn't [turn] wild.

43. 닉과 주디는 최고의 속임수를 썼거든요.
He and Judy had pulled their greatest [trick].

44. 그들은 세럼을 블루베리 주스로 바꿔 놓았던 거예요.
They had [switch with]ed the serum with blueberry juice.

Word Box

sank	lock up	predator	dart	corner
sink(주저앉다)의 과거형	철창 안에 가두다	몡 포식자	몡 (작은) 화살	통 (궁지에) 몰아넣다
switch with	turn	trick	expect	
~와 바꾸다	통 ~한 상태로 변하다	몡 속임수	통 예상하다	

45 닉과 주디는 보고 서장에게 증거를 제출했고, 벨웨더는 체포되었어요.

Nick and Judy gave the evidence to Chief Bogo, and Bellwether was [arrest]ed.

46 오터튼 씨를 포함해 야만스럽게 변했던 모든 동물들은 곧 치유될 거였어요.

All the animals who had gone savage—including Mr. Otterton—would soon be [cure]d.

47 주디와 닉은 사건을 해결했고, 그들이 어리석은 토끼나 교활한 여우 이상의 훌륭한 존재라는 것을 증명했어요.

Judy and Nick had solved the case, and proved that they were far more than a dumb bunny and a [sly] fox.

48 그들은 파트너이자 가장 친한 친구였고, 주토피아의 범죄와 싸울 준비가 되었어요!

They were [partner]s—and best friends—ready to fight crime in Zootopia!

Word Box

cure	sly	partner	arrest
통 치유하다	형 교활한	명 파트너	통 체포하다

FROZEN 2

빈칸에 알맞은 단어를 채워 문장을 완성하세요.

1 아렌델 왕국의 안나와 엘사는 어린 시절 엄마가 불러주던 자장가를 매우 좋아했어요.

In the kingdom of Arendelle, Anna and Elsa loved the _____ their mother sang to them when they were children.

2 그 자장가는 비밀의 강에 관한 노래였는데, 과거에 대한 모든 답을 담고 있었어요.

The lullaby was about a secret river, which held all the answers about the _____.

3 그 노래는 생각할 거리를 많이 주었고, 상상력을 불러일으켰어요.

It gave the girls a lot to think about and excited their _____s.

4 시간이 흐르면서 안나와 엘사는 더 성장했어요. 엘사는 눈과 얼음을 마음대로 쓸 수 있는 마법을 발견했고, 그것은 점점 더 강해졌어요.

As time went on, Anna and Elsa grew older. Elsa _____ed her magical power over snow and ice, which became stronger and stronger.

5 어느 날 밤, 신비로운 목소리가 그녀를 불렀어요. 그것은 무엇을 원하는 걸까요?

One night, a _____ voice called to her. What did it want?

6 엘사는 그 목소리가 자신이 북쪽으로 가는 것을 원한다는 사실을 깨달았어요.

Elsa realized that the voice wanted her to travel _____.

7 그녀는 피오르드로 가서 엄청난 얼음 돌풍을 쏘았어요.

She went to the fjord and _____ out an enormous icy blast.

8 엘사의 마법이 새롭고 강력한 무언가를 해낸 것은 분명했어요. 하지만 이것은 무슨 의미일까요?

It was _____ that Elsa's magic had done something new and powerful. But what did it mean?

Word Box

discover	lullaby	imagination	past
동 발견하다	명 자장가	명 상상력	명 과거
clear	shot	north	mysterious
형 분명한	shoot(쏘다)의 과거형	부 북쪽으로	형 신비로운

⑨ 엘사가 일으킨 돌풍이 마법에 걸린 숲의 정령들을 깨웠다는 사실을 알려주기 위해 트롤들이 절벽을 올라 왔어요.

The trolls rolled up to the cliffs to let Elsa know that her blast had _____ed the spirits of the Enchanted Forest.

⑩ 트롤들은 그녀에게 정령들이 화가 났다고 경고했어요.

They _____ed her that the spirits were angry.

⑪ 그 숲은 노덜드라라고 하는 유목 부족이 사는 곳으로도 알려져 있었어요.

The forest was also where a _____ group of people called the Northuldra were said to live.

⑫ 엘사는 마음 깊이 알고 있었어요. 그 신비한 목소리를 따라 마법에 걸린 숲으로 가야 한다는 것을요.

Elsa knew in her heart that she must follow the mysterious voice to the _____ Forest.

⑬ 안나와 그녀의 친구인 크리스토프와 올라프, 그리고 스벤도 엘사와 함께 갔어요.

Anna and her friends Kristoff, Olaf, and Sven _____ with Elsa.

⑭ 숲에서 그들은 그들 주변을 '쉭' 소리내며 지나가는 바람의 정령을 만났어요.

In the forest, they met the Wind Spirit, who _____ed around them.

⑮ 그들은 노덜드라 사람들도 만났어요. 그들은 이야기를 해주었고, 엘사와 안나, 그리고 그들의 친구들과 다른 점보다는 비슷한 점이 더 많다는 사실도 드러냈어요.

They also met the Northuldra people, who told them stories and revealed that they were more _____ to Elsa, Anna, and their friends than they were different.

⑯ 엘사와 친구들이 노덜드라 족을 알아가는 동안, 강력한 불의 정령이 나타나 마법에 걸린 숲에 불을 질렀어요!

While Elsa and her friends were getting to know the Northuldra, the _____ Fire Spirit appeared and set the Enchanted Forest on fire!

Word Box

mighty	nomadic	enchanted	warn
형 강력한	형 유목의	형 마법에 걸린	동 경고하다
similar	whoosh	went	awaken
형 비슷한	동 '쉭' 소리를 내며 지나가다	go(가다)의 과거형	동 깨우다

⑰ 엘사는 마법으로 불이 번지는 것을 막으려 했지만 소용이 없었어요.

Elsa tried to stop the [____]ing fire with her magic, but it wasn't working.

⑱ 크리스토프는 안나와 순록이 불을 피해 탈출하도록 도왔어요.

Kristoff helped Anna and the [____] escape the flames.

⑲ 마침내 엘사는 불의 정령에게 눈송이를 먹여서 그를 진정시킬 수 있었어요.

Elsa was finally able to calm the Fire Spirit by [____]ing it snowflakes.

⑳ 불의 정령은 작은 도롱뇽이었어요.

The Fire Spirit was actually a little [____].

㉑ 엘사는 목소리를 다시 들었고, 불의 정령도 그 소리를 들을 수 있다는 것을 알게 됐어요.

Elsa heard the voice again, and she [____]d that the Fire Spirit could hear it, too.

㉒ 엘사는 더이상 머물러 있을 수 없었어요. 그녀는 여정을 계속해야 했어요.

Elsa couldn't stay any longer. She had to [____] her journey.

㉓ 안나와 올라프가 그녀와 함께 했고, 크리스토프와 스벤은 노덜드라 족과 함께 남았어요.

Anna and Olaf [____]ed her, while Kristoff and Sven stayed behind with the Northuldra.

㉔ 북쪽으로 향하던 중, 안나와 엘사는 부모님이 탔던 난파선을 발견했어요!

Heading north, Anna and Elsa discovered their parent's [____]!

㉕ 그들은 배 안에서 지도를 살펴보고, 부모님이 북쪽으로 여행했던 이유는 엘사가 왜 마법을 갖게 되었는지 알기 위함이었다는 사실을 알게 되었어요.

Inside the ship, they studied a map and learned that their parents had [____]ed north to understand why Elsa had magic.

㉖ 엘사는 부모님을 잃은 것처럼 안나를 잃게 될까 봐 두려웠어요.

Elsa [____]ed losing Anna, just as she had lost their parents.

Word Box

continue	fear	notice	salamander	feed
통 계속하다	통 두려워하다	통 알아차리다	명 도롱뇽	통 먹이다
spread	travel	shipwreck	join	reindeer
통 번지다	통 여행하다	명 난파선	통 함께 하다	명 순록

27. 엘사는 남은 여행을 혼자 하기로 결심했어요.

Elsa decided to make the rest of the journey ☐.

28. 엘사는 무거운 마음으로 얼음 보트를 만들어서 안나와 올라프를 재빨리 들어올려 태우고는 그들을 안전하게 떠나 보냈어요.

With a heavy heart, Elsa formed a boat made of ice that ☐ed up Anna and Olaf and carried them safely away.

29. 안나와 올라프는 크게 항의했지만, 안나가 실수로 배의 방향을 잠자는 땅의 거인들을 향해 가도록 만든 후에는 배를 세울 방법이 없었어요.

Anna and Olaf loudly ☐ed, but there was no way they could stop the boat after Anna accidentally steered it toward the sleeping Earth Giants.

30. 안나와 올라프는 그들을 지나칠 때 조용한 상태를 유지했어요.

Anna and Olaf kept ☐ as they passed them.

31. 그 어느 때보다도 단단히 결심한 채로, 엘사는 여정의 다음 단계인 검은 바다에 도착했어요. 이제 그녀는 그 바다를 건너야 했어요.

More ☐ than ever, Elsa reached the next part of her journey: the Dark Sea. Now she needed to cross it.

32. 물의 정령 노크가 바다에서 솟아 올라 엘사를 막으려 했어요.

The Water Nokk ☐ed up from the sea and tried to stop Elsa.

33. 맹렬한 전투 끝에, 엘사와 노크는 서로의 힘이 동등하다는 것을 깨달았어요.

After a fierce battle, Elsa and the Water Nokk realized that their powers were ☐.

34. 그들 사이에 서로를 존중하는 마음이 생겼어요.

A mutual ☐ formed between them.

Word Box

alone	rear	quiet	protest
형 부 혼자, 외로운	동 우뚝 솟다	형 조용한	동 항의하다
scoop	determined	equal	respect
동 재빨리 들어올리다	형 단단히 결심한	형 동등한	명 존경, 존중

54

35 한편 안나와 올라프의 여정은 동굴 속으로 이어졌어요. 그들 앞에 얼음 조각상 하나가 나타났어요.

Meanwhile, Anna and Olaf's journey continued into a cave, where an ice _____ appeared in front of them.

36 그것은 엘사로부터 온 신호였어요. 그 여정은 여왕의 몇 가지 질문들에 대답한 것이었어요.

It was a signal from Elsa. The journey had _____ ed some of the queen's questions.

37 엘사는 마침내 북쪽에 도착했어요!

Elsa had finally _____ d in the north!

38 그녀를 부르던 목소리는 이제 조용해져 속삭임이 되었어요. 엘사는 그 목소리가 지금까지 계속 그녀의 내면에 있었다는 사실을 깨달았어요.

The voice that had called to her now quieted to a _____ , and she realized it had been within her all along.

39 그것은 엘사가 내면의 평화를 발견하도록 그녀를 인도했던 거예요.

It had _____ d her to discover her inner peace.

40 자매는 함께 힘을 합쳐 마침내 아렌델 왕국에 평화와 조화를 다시 회복시켰어요.

By working together, the sisters were able to _____ peace and harmony to the land at last.

Word Box

whisper	answer	arrive	sculpture
명 속삭임	동 대답하다	동 도착하다	명 조각상
restore	guide		
동 회복시키다	동 인도하다		

Practice Book

Part 1 단어 연습 (Word Practice)

스토리북에 등장한 핵심 어휘를 익힙니다. 어려운 단어들을 순서대로 정리해 보고,
이 외에도 잘 모르는 단어는 사전에서 찾아 뜻과 철자를 기록합니다.

Part 2 전체 문장 연습 (Sentence Practice)

읽은 내용을 다시 떠올리며 우리말에 맞도록 문장을 완성합니다.
빈칸에 들어갈 알맞은 단어를 찾는 과정에서 문장 구조와 표현을 익힐 수 있습니다.

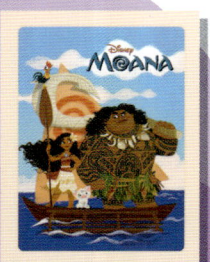 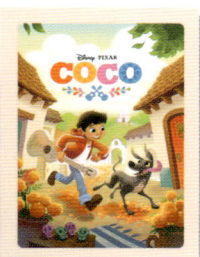   

Copyright©2022 Disney Enterprises, Inc. and Pixar. All rights reserved.